PREFACE

Although probability is included in the NCTM Standards, it's a topic that doesn't get much attention in the primary grades. There are two reasons for this. One is that instructional materials aimed at teaching young children about probability haven't been available. Another is that primary teachers typically haven't had much experience with probability and therefore don't feel comfortable teaching it.

Math By All Means: Probability, Grades 1–2 by Bonnie Tank addresses both of these issues. The unit provides for five to six weeks of instruction and was tested extensively in actual classroom settings. Not only does the unit give specific and complete information about how to introduce activities, lead classroom discussions, and assess children's understanding, it also is a useful vehicle for helping teachers learn about probability along with their students.

Bonnie is well qualified to write this unit. She has more than 25 years of experience teaching both children and teachers. She knows what kinds of activities engage children and help them make sense of complex ideas. She understands how to structure lessons so that they're accessible to students and also manageable in the classroom. She knows how to encourage and support teachers to try new teaching ideas. Bonnie brought all of this expertise to writing this unit.

Before Bonnie tackled writing this unit, she and I taught it several times in different classes over a three-year period. During that time, we made changes in the lessons and tinkered with the activities. Also, Bonnie asked for feedback from teachers in the San Francisco Bay Area and the Tucson Unified School District Chapter 1 Mathematics Project who tested the unit in their classrooms. This book presents the activities that Bonnie felt were most successful in the classroom and would be successful for other teachers.

All of the "From the Classroom" vignettes included in this unit draw from Bonnie's experiences while teaching the unit to second graders. However, the grade level span assigned to the unit indicates that it's suitable for both grades one and two. The activities are designed so that they're accessible to younger children and students with limited ability, while having the depth to challenge more interested and capable math students.

I'm pleased to present this unit and, as always, am interested in your feedback.

Marilyn Burns
October 1995

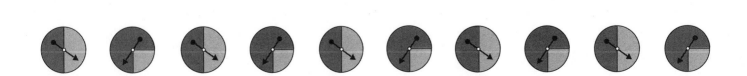

MATH
By All Means®

PROBABILITY
Grades 1–2

by Bonnie Tank
A MARILYN BURNS REPLACEMENT UNIT

MATH SOLUTIONS PUBLICATIONS

Editorial Direction: Lorri Ungaretti
Art direction and design: Aileen Friedman
Typesetting: Rad H. M. Proctor
Illustrations: David Healy, First Image
Cover background and border designs: Barbara Gelfand

Marilyn Burns Education Associates is dedicated to improving mathematics education. For information about Math Solutions inservice workshops and courses, resource materials, and other services, write or call:

Marilyn Burns Education Associates
150 Gate 5 Road, Suite 101
Sausalito, CA 94965
Telephone: (800) 868-9092 or (415) 332-4181
Fax: (415) 331-1931

Web site: http://www.mathsolutions.com

ISBN 0-941355-15-2

This book is printed on recycled paper (at least 50% post-consumer waste).

A MESSAGE FROM MARILYN BURNS

This book is part of a larger effort by Marilyn Burns Education Associates to publish teacher resources and provide inservice courses and workshops. In 1984, we began offering **Math Solutions** five-day courses and one-day workshops nationwide, now attended by more than 60,000 teachers and administrators in 34 states. Our goal, then and now, has been to help teachers improve how they teach mathematics to students in kindergarten through grade 8. Since 1987, we have also published books as a way to support and extend the experiences provided at our courses and workshops.

Following are brief descriptions of the various **Math Solutions** courses, workshops, and publications currently available. Books may be obtained through educational catalogs or at your local teacher bookstore. For further information about inservice programs and to learn how MBEA works in partnership with school districts, regional consortia, and state education departments to improve mathematics instruction, please call us at **(800) 868-9092.** Or visit our Web site: **http://www.mathsolutions.com**

MATH SOLUTIONS INSERVICE COURSES AND WORKSHOPS

Five-Day Summer Courses

Teachers are the key to improving classroom mathematics instruction. Math Solutions intensive, weeklong staff development courses help teachers develop new classroom outlooks and skills.

- **Math Solutions, Level 1 (K–8)** presents practical and proven ways to help teachers implement the NCTM standards.

- **Math Solutions, Level 2 (K–8)** is a continuation of Level 1 with an emphasis on making assessment and student writing integral to math instruction.

- **Math Solutions, Level 3 (K–8)** provides an extended look at the challenges of teaching mathematics. Participants learn how to organize instruction into curriculum units. Two versions are available:

  Learning More Mathematics. This course offers an in-depth investigation of the mathematics in the lessons teachers teach to their students.

  Preparing Teacher Leaders. This course is for school districts that want to increase their capacity to support the improvement of classroom math teaching.

One-Day Workshops

These workshops build teachers' interest in improving their mathematics teaching and provide follow-up support for teachers who have attended inservice programs. They are tailored specifically to the particular needs of schools and districts.

- **Introducing Problem Solving**
  The Way to Math Solutions (K–8)
  Math for Middle School (Grades 6–8)
  Developing Number Sense (Grades 3–8)

- **Integrating Math and Language Arts**
  Math and Literature (K–3, 4–6, or K–6)
  Writing in Math Class (Grades 2–8)

- **Teaching with Manipulative Materials**
  For any materials and any K–6 grade range

- **Teaching with Replacement Units**
  Money (Grades 1–2)
  Place Value (Grades 1–2)
  Multiplication (Grades 2–4)
  Division (Grades 3–4)
  Geometry (Grades 1–2, 3–4, or 1–4)
  Probability (Grades 1–2, 3–5, or 1–5)

- **Working with District Math Teams**
  Preparing Teacher Leaders (K–8)
  Math Solutions for School-Based Change (K–8)
  Conference for Administrators (K–8)

(over, please)

MATH SOLUTIONS PUBLICATIONS

General Interest

It's important for educators to communicate with parents about math education issues. Here are two excellent ways to do so.

- **Math: Facing an American Phobia** by Marilyn Burns
- **Mathematics: What Are You Teaching My Child?,** a videotape with Marilyn Burns

Resource Books for Problem Solving

These books bring to teachers a vision of teaching mathematics through problem solving. They set the standard for professional teaching resources by stimulating, inspiring, and supporting teachers to translate the NCTM standards into actual classroom instruction.

- **About Teaching Mathematics** by Marilyn Burns
- **50 Problem-Solving Lessons: The Best from 10 Years of Math Solutions Newsletters** by Marilyn Burns
- **A Collection of Math Lessons from Grades 1 through 3** by Marilyn Burns and Bonnie Tank
- **A Collection of Math Lessons from Grades 3 through 6** by Marilyn Burns
- **A Collection of Math Lessons from Grades 6 through 8** by Marilyn Burns and Cathy Humphreys

Linking Mathematics and Language Arts

The first book in the list below explains why students should write in math class, describes different types of writing assignments, and offers teaching tips and suggestions. The other three books show teachers how to use children's literature to introduce important math ideas to elementary students.

- **Writing in Math Class: A Resource for Grades 2–8** by Marilyn Burns
- **Math and Literature (K–3), Book One** by Marilyn Burns
- **Math and Literature (K–3), Book Two** by Stephanie Sheffield
- **Math and Literature (Grades 4–6)** by Rusty Bresser

Math Replacement Units

Designed as an alternative to textbook instruction, each *Math By All Means* Replacement Unit presents a cohesive plan for five to six weeks of classroom instruction. The units focus on thinking and reasoning, incorporate the use of manipulative materials, and provide opportunities for students to communicate about their learning.

- **Math By All Means: Money, Grades 1–2** by Jane Crawford
- **Math By All Means: Place Value, Grades 1–2** by Marilyn Burns
- **Math By All Means: Geometry, Grades 1–2** by Chris Confer
- **Math By All Means: Probability, Grades 1–2** by Bonnie Tank
- **Math By All Means: Multiplication, Grade 3** by Marilyn Burns
- **Math By All Means: Division, Grades 3–4** by Susan Ohanian and Marilyn Burns
- **Math By All Means: Geometry, Grades 3–4** by Cheryl Rectanus
- **Math By All Means: Probability, Grades 3–4** by Marilyn Burns
- **Math By All Means: Area and Perimeter, Grades 5–6** by Cheryl Rectanus

Books for Children

For more than 20 years, I've brought my math message directly to children, beginning with *The I Hate Mathematics! Book,* first published in 1974. In 1994, I launched the Marilyn Burns Brainy Day Books series.

- **Spaghetti and Meatballs for All!** by Marilyn Burns
- **The Greedy Triangle** by Marilyn Burns
- **The King's Commissioners** by Aileen Friedman
- **A Cloak for the Dreamer** by Aileen Friedman
- **The $1.00 Word Riddle Book** by Marilyn Burns
- **The I Hate Mathematics! Book** by Marilyn Burns
- **The Book of Think** by Marilyn Burns
- **Math for Smarty Pants** by Marilyn Burns

Acknowledgments

Special thanks for the insight and support provided by the students, teachers, parents, and principals with whom this unit was developed and tested.

Jefferson Elementary School, San Francisco Unified School District, San Francisco, California
    Judith Rosen, Principal
    Ruth Cunningham
    Darcie Chan
    Joyce Fong
    Patrick Mulkeen

Alamo School, San Francisco Unified School District, San Francisco, California
    Dorothy Quinones, Principal
    Joyce Bullentini
    Marge Tsukamoto

Wildwood School, Piedmont, California
    Carolyn Raffo, Principal
    Nancy Litton
    Jade Shirachi

Tucson Unified School District, Tucson, Arizona
    Carol Brooks and the teachers in the Title I/Exxon Mathematics/Science Project.

Exxon Education Foundation for providing the support for my work with teachers at Jefferson Elementary School and for encouraging me to write this unit.

This book is dedicated to Doug and Josh Haner.

CONTENTS

INTRODUCTION

One morning, as the class was settling into a game I had just introduced, Natalya ran up to me, followed meekly by her partner, Dean.

"Who goes first?" she asked excitedly. "He always goes first."

"What would be a fair way to decide?" I asked calmly.

"We were going to roll the dice," Dean said quietly.

"How would that help you decide?" I asked.

"Whoever get the highest goes first," Dean responded.

"But he always goes first!" said Natalya, rather agitated.

"You each roll, and I'll watch," I suggested.

Natalya rolled a 4; Dean rolled a 3. They returned to their seats.

I could tell that Natalya was satisfied but not convinced. Her experience had not led her to the conclusion that each person had an equal chance of rolling a higher number on one die.

Those of us teaching young children have experienced many situations in which children have to decide who goes first—who's first to get a drink, who's up first in kick ball, who's first in line at the cafeteria.

When I asked the students in my class how they might decide who goes first, they had many ideas:

Spin a spinner to see who gets the highest number.

Play the card game War.

Pick the highest card.

Play ro sham bo (another name for scissors, paper, rock).

Play tic-tac-toe.

Draw straws.

Roll a die.

Play a game like checkers.

Some of the methods children use they learn from playmates or older siblings. They also learn methods from adults who try to help them find ways to solve conflicts. Intuitively, children sense that the methods are fair ways to choose, but most first and second grade children have not had the opportunity to consider these methods from the mathematical perspective of probability.

Goals for Probability Instruction

This unit provides teachers with a plan for including probability in first and second grade mathematics instruction. Understanding of the basic ideas of probability and statistics develops gradually for students as a result of many experiences. Experiences in first and second grade form the foundation for later understanding.

The activities in this unit suggest ways to involve children in thinking about the following basic concepts:

■ **Some events are more likely than others, while some events are equally likely. Students are usually familiar with this idea informally.** The activities in the unit build on that informal understanding, connect it to the standard language of probability, and provide additional experiences.

■ **Probability is evident in our everyday lives.** Children have some informal understanding of probability from their real-life experiences. They're used to hearing weather reports and have a feel for what it means to have an 80 percent chance of rain. They know about rolling dice or playing a card game to make decisions, and they've probably had experience using spinners or dice in games. This unit builds on students' past experiences and engages them with a variety of games, activities, and investigations in which they predict outcomes and then test their predictions.

■ **In a fair game, both players have an equal chance of winning.** Children have an intuitive sense about the fairness of games. This unit provides experiences in which students informally test their ideas about fairness by playing and evaluating games and by inventing and evaluating their own games.

■ **You can use a sample set of data to predict an outcome.** Surveys are frequently used to determine what people think about an issue or an idea. Of course, those who gather information, called surveyors or pollsters, don't ask everyone for an opinion. Instead, they use the information from a small number of people to make a prediction about the entire population. Similarly, in this unit, students take samples and use the information they gather to make predictions.

■ **Larger sample sets of data give more reliable information than do smaller sample sets.** If you spin a spinner that is half red and half blue 10 times, it would be unlikely to land on each color exactly 5 times. If it landed on blue 6 times, that would reflect a 60 percent outcome for blue, although the theory predicts a 50 percent outcome. However, with a

larger sample, say of 100 spins, blue would come up closer to 50 percent of the time. In several activities in the unit, students compare class data to their individual samples. They learn that larger sets of data provide more reliable information for verifying or challenging their predictions or theories.

Students encounter these ideas throughout the unit. They play games and examine what makes a game fair or unfair. They learn that some games are based on chance, some on strategy, and some on both. Using dice, cards, and spinners, children analyze events that are equally likely and events that are more likely than others. Through the investigations in the unit, children make predictions, collect data, and reflect on results.

While involved in the probability experiments, students have opportunities throughout the unit to develop number sense and reinforce computation skills through such experiences as adding two numbers on dice or cards, finding their scores in games, totaling results from whole class statistics, and keeping track of the number of times they spin a spinner.

The Materials

The activities in the unit call for using dice, playing cards, tiles, and spinners. Students use dice and tiles for several games in the unit and also to collect data. They use playing cards to determine the likelihood of getting different sums when randomly turning over two cards. They explore results from experiments with two different spinners—one that is divided equally into two regions and another with one region larger than the other.

What's in the Unit?

This five- to six-week unit on probability was created to respond to the recommendations for mathematics instruction presented in the National Council of Teachers of Mathematics' *Curriculum and Evaluation Standards for School Mathematics* (NCTM, 1989). The unit gives children a variety of experiences that involve them in thinking about some of the basic ideas of probability. Through a collection of hands-on games and experiments, students explore the likelihood of events, use data to make predictions about outcomes, and determine whether games are fair.

The activities are structured so that they are accessible to children with limited math experience and ability while also having the potential to challenge students with more interest and aptitude for mathematics. For all children, the variety of games and investigations provides a base of experience on which they later build a deeper understanding of probability.

During the unit, children participate in whole class lessons, work cooperatively in pairs or small groups, and do an assortment of independent activities. Writing is an integral part of their math learning. Homework is used to further students' classroom experiences as well as to communicate with parents about their children's learning.

The Structure of This Book

This unit is organized into four main areas: *Whole Class Lessons, Menu Activities, Assessments,* and *Homework.* Blackline masters and recording sheets needed for activities are also included.

Whole Class Lessons

Six whole class lessons, each requiring one to two class periods, give the students a common set of experiences on which to build their learning about probability. The first lesson introduces children to probability as part of their everyday lives and presents some of the language they will use throughout the unit. Four lessons use dice, playing cards, or spinners to engage children with basic ideas about probability. In one lesson, children examine the basic addition facts and discuss strategies for determining their sums.

The instructional directions for each lesson are presented in four sections:

Overview gives a brief description of the lesson.

Before the lesson outlines the preparation needed before teaching the lesson.

Teaching directions provides step-by-step instructions for presenting the lesson.

From the classroom describes what happened when the lesson was taught to one class of second graders. This vignette helps bring alive the instructional guidelines by giving an over-the-shoulder look into a classroom, telling how lessons were organized, how students reacted, and how the teacher responded. The vignettes are not standards of what "should" happen but a record of what did happen with one class.

Menu Activities

The menu is a collection of activities that children do independently—in pairs, in groups, or individually. Menu activities pose problems, set up situations, and ask questions that give children a variety of experiences with probability. Most of the tasks on the menu do not build conceptually on one another and therefore do not need to be done in any particular sequence. Also, the tasks are designed so that students can do them several times, thus continuing to explore ideas by returning to activities that interest them.

The unit contains eight menu activities: five require students to work with partners, and three are designed to be done individually.

The instructional directions for each menu activity are presented in four sections:

Overview gives a brief description of the activity.

Before the lesson outlines the preparation needed before presenting the activity.

Getting started provides instructions for introducing the activity.

From the classroom describes what happened when the activity was introduced to one class of second graders. As with the whole class lessons, the vignette gives a view into an actual classroom, describing how the teacher gave directions and how the students responded.

For additional information about using menus, see the introduction to the menu activities on page 69.

Assessments

This unit offers six assessments. They are listed in the Table of Contents and placed near the activities from which they evolve. Also, they are identified in the book by gray bars in the margins.

For specific information about assessing understanding, see the introduction to the Assessments section on page 63.

Homework

Homework assignments have two purposes: They extend the work students do in class, and they inform parents about the instruction their child is getting. Suggestions for homework assignments and ways to communicate with parents are included in the Homework section.

Blackline Masters

Blackline masters are included for all menu activities and recording sheets.

Notes about Classroom Organization

Setting the Stage for Cooperation

Throughout much of the unit, students are asked to work cooperatively with a partner or small group. Interaction is an important ingredient for children's intellectual development. They learn from interaction with one another as well as with adults.

Teachers who have taught the unit have reported different systems for organizing children to work cooperatively. Some put pairs of numbers in a bag and have children draw to choose partners. Some assign partners. Some have seatmates work together. Others let children pick their own partners.

Some teachers have students work with the same partner for the entire unit. Others let children choose partners for each activity, allowing them either to change frequently or stay with the same person. Some don't have children work with specific partners but instead with others who have chosen the same activity.

The system for organizing children matters less than the underlying classroom attitude. What's important is that children are encouraged to work together, listen to one another's ideas, and be willing to help classmates. Students should see their classroom as a place where cooperation and collaboration are valued and expected. This does not mean, of course, that children never work individually. However, it does respect the principle that interaction fosters learning and, therefore, that cooperation is basic to the culture of the classroom.

A System for the Menu Activities

Teachers report several different ways of organizing the menu activities. Some teachers use a copy machine to enlarge the blackline masters of the menu tasks onto 11-by-17-inch paper, mount them on construction paper or tagboard, and post them. Although the teacher introduces each activity to the entire class, individual students can refer later to the posted directions for clarification. (Note: A set of posters with menu activity directions is available for purchase from Cuisenaire Company of America.)

Rather than enlarge and post the tasks, other teachers duplicate a half dozen of each and make them available for children to take to their seats. Mounting the tasks on tagboard makes the copies more durable. Some teachers put the tasks in booklets, making one for each child or pair of students. For any of the above alternatives, children take materials from the general supply and return them when they finish their work or at the end of class.

Some teachers prefer to assign different locations in the classroom for different tasks. For each activity, they place a copy of the task and the worksheets and materials needed in a cardboard carton or rubber tub. At the beginning of menu time, monitors distribute the tubs to the assigned locations. The number of chairs at each location determines the number of children who can work there.

Each of these systems encourages children to be independent and responsible for their learning. They are allowed to spend the amount of time they need on any one task and make choices about the sequence in which they work on tasks. Also, the tasks are designed for children to do over and over again, avoiding the situation where a child is "finished" and has nothing to do.

How Children Record

Teachers also use different procedures to organize the way children record for activities. Some prepare a booklet for each child, making covers either by folding 12-by-18-inch sheets of construction paper in half or by using regular file folders, and require children to record individually even when working cooperatively. Some teachers prepare booklets for partners and have the partners collaborate on their written work. Other teachers don't use booklets but have students record on separate sheets of paper and place their finished work in an in basket.

Some teachers have children copy the list of menu activities and keep track of what they do by putting a check by an activity each time they do it. Other teachers give children a list of the menu activities by duplicating the blackline master on page 170. It's important that the recording system is clear to the class and helps the teacher keep track of the children's progress.

About Writing in Math Class

For both learning activities and assessments, teachers must rely on children's writing to get insights into their thinking. Helping children learn to describe their reasoning processes, and become comfortable doing so, is extremely important and requires planning and attention. Experience and encouragement are two major ingredients.

It's important for children to know that their writing is important because it helps the teacher learn about how they are thinking. Teachers need to reinforce over and over again that the teacher is the audience for students' writing, so the students need to provide sufficient details to make their thinking and reasoning processes clear.

For children who have difficulty with writing, it may be helpful at times to take their dictation or provide a tape recorder for them to use to explain their ideas.

Managing Materials and Supplies

Teachers who have taught this unit planned time at the beginning of the year for children to explore the concrete materials they would use in their math learning throughout the year. Also, all the teachers gave their students guidelines for the care and storage of materials. The following materials and supplies are needed for this unit:

Materials

- Dice, two per child
- Playing cards, one deck per pair of children
- Color Tiles (1-inch square tiles in four colors), one set of 400
- Small plastic bowls or baskets large enough to hold 20 tiles, one per pair of children
- Interlocking (Multilink, Snap, or Unifix) cubes, 10 blue and 10 red per child
- Plastic straws, about 12
- 5-by-8-inch index cards, at least one per child

General Classroom Supplies

- Ample supply of paper, including chart paper, tagboard, white construction paper, lined newsprint, and writing paper
- Scissors, at least one per pair of children
- Tape
- 3-by-3 inch and $1\frac{1}{2}$-by-2-inch Post-it Notes
- Paper clips

In addition, recording sheets for individual activities are included in the Blackline Masters section. Most teachers choose to have supplies of each sheet available for children to take when needed.

A Comment about Calculators

It's assumed that during this unit, and in the classroom throughout the year, calculators are as available to the children as pencils, paper, rulers, and other general classroom supplies. You may occasionally ask students not to use calculators if you want to know about their ability to deal with numbers on their own. However, such times should be the exception rather than the rule. Children should regard calculators as tools that are generally available for their use when doing mathematics.

As with other materials, children need time to become familiar with calculators. Some children will find them fascinating and useful; others will not be interested in or comfortable with using them.

A Suggested Daily Schedule

It's helpful to think through the entire unit and make an overall teaching plan. However, it isn't possible to predict how a class will respond as the unit progresses, and adjustments and changes will most likely be required. The following day-to-day schedule is a suggested five-week guide. It offers a plan that varies the pace of daily instruction, interweaving whole class lessons with independent work on menu activities. The schedule also suggests times for discussing menu activities and giving homework assignments.

Day 1   Whole Class Lesson: Likely–Unlikely

Discuss probability with the students. Introduce the *Likely–Unlikely* lesson. Have children write likely and unlikely statements.

Day 2   Whole Class Lesson: Likely–Unlikely (continued)

The children write their likely and unlikely statements on large strips of paper and present them to the class.

Day 3   Whole Class Lesson: Empty the Bowl

Introduce the *Empty the Bowl* lesson. Have the children play the game and write their results on the class chart. At the end of the period, discuss the data. Give homework assignment: *Empty the Bowl*.

Day 4   Whole Class Lesson: Is It 10?

Begin class by having children record on the class chart their results from playing *Empty the Bowl* at home. Discuss the data. Then introduce *Is It 10?* Give the children time to play the game and record data on the class chart. Shortly before the end of class, initiate a class discussion about the results. Sometime during the day, have the children prepare menu folders and lists of menu tasks.

Day 5   Introduce Menu Activities: Empty the Bowl with 20, Is It 12?

Present the directions for the menu activities *Empty the Bowl with 20* and *Is It 12?* Have students choose menu activities to work on. (If they didn't make menu folders and menu lists the previous day, have them do so now.)

Day 6   Introduce Menu Activity: Likely–Unlikely Book

Present the directions for *Likely–Unlikely Book*. Students choose menu activities to work on for the remainder of the class.

Day 7   Whole Class Lesson: Addition Facts and Strategies, Part 1

Introduce Part 1 of the *Addition Facts and Strategies* lesson. For the remainder of the period, students work on menu activities. Direct the students to post their data for *Is It 12?* At the end of the period, give homework assignment: *Is It 12?*

Day 8 **Whole Class Lesson: Addition Facts and Strategies, Part 2**

Begin class by having children record on a class chart their results from playing *Is It 12?* at home. Discuss the data. Then continue discussing strategies for adding with Part 2 of the lesson. For the remainder of the period, students work on menu activities.

Day 9 **Whole Class Lesson: Spinner Experiment**

Introduce the *Spinner Experiment.* The children make spinners and collect data. As a class, discuss the results, then ask students to write about them.

Day 10 **Assessment: Strategies for 7 + 6**

Have children write about three ways to find the answer to 7 + 6. Then students choose and work on activities from the menu. Direct students to complete *Empty the Bowl with 20* and post their data for class discussion at the beginning of the next day's class.

Day 11 **Introduce Menu Activity: Roll One Die**

Begin class by discussing the children's results from *Empty the Bowl with 20.* Then introduce *Roll One Die.* For the remainder of the period, students work on menu activities.

Day 12 **Introduce Menu Activity: More Spinners**

Present the directions for *More Spinners.* For the rest of the period, students work on menu activities.

Day 13 **Assessment: When You Turn Over Two Cards**

Have children review the class data from *Is It 10?* and *Is It 12?* and then do the assessment. When they complete the assessment, they continue to work on menu activities.

Day 14 **Assessment: Likely and Unlikely**

Review probability terminology introduced so far and have children write about what *likely* and *unlikely* mean. When children complete the assessment, they work on menu activities.

Day 15 **Menu**

Students continue working on menu activities. Direct students to complete *Roll One Die* for class discussion at the beginning of the next day's class.

Day 16 **Introduce Menu Activity: Roll Two Dice**

Begin class with children discussing and combining their data from *Roll One Die.* Introduce the menu activity *Roll Two Dice.* Then let students choose and work on activities from the menu.

Day 17 **Menu**

Students continue working on menu activities. Direct students to complete their experiments from *More Spinners* so they can discuss the results at the end of the period. Discuss *More Spinners* as a class.

Day 18   Assessment: 100 Spins

Ask children to predict what will happen if they spin the spinner 100 times. After discussing their predictions, have them write about their ideas. Then they choose menu activities. Give homework assignment: *Spinners.*

Day 19   Whole Class Lesson: The Plus and Minus Game, Part 1

Introduce *The Plus and Minus Game* lesson. Have children play the game and write letters. If time allows, discuss the game with the class and have volunteers read their letters.

Day 20   Whole Class Lesson: The Plus and Minus Game, Part 2

Teach *The New Plus and Minus Game,* and have students collect data for discussion.

Day 21   Introduce Menu Activity: The 1 to 10 Game

Have children work in groups of four to combine their data from Day 18's homework assignment. Discuss the data as a class. Introduce the menu activity *The 1 to 10 Game.* Continue work on menu activities. Remind the children to enter their results from *Roll Two Dice* on the class chart so they can participate in a class discussion tomorrow.

Day 22   Menu

Discuss the class data from *Roll Two Dice.* Then students continue working on menu activities. Give homework assignment: *Roll Two Dice.*

Day 23   Assessment: When You Roll Two Dice

Begin with a discussion of the children's experiences playing *Roll Two Dice* at home. Present the *When You Roll Two Dice* assessment. When children complete the assessment, they choose menu activities to work on for the remainder of the class. Give homework assignment: *The 1 to 10 Game.*

Day 24   Introduce Menu Activity: Invent a Game

Begin with a discussion of the children's experiences playing *The 1 to 10 Game* at home and in class. Introduce the activity *Invent a Game.* Then children choose and work on activities from the menu.

Day 25   Menu

Continue work on menu. Remind children to complete the *Likely–Unlikely Book* menu activity so their books can be shared in the class library.

Day 26   Assessment: Agree or Disagree with Sara

Present the *Agree or Disagree with Sara* assessment. When children complete the assessment, they choose menu activities to work on.

Day 27   Menu

Direct students to put finishing touches on invented games. Encourage children to read Likely–Unlikely books written by their classmates.

Day 28 **Culminating Activity: Game Day**

Half of the students share their invented games with the rest of the class.

Day 29 **Culminating Activity: Game Day (continued)**

The remaining students share their invented games.

Letter to Parents

Although parents learn about their children's experiences from homework assignments and papers sent home, you may want to give them general information about the unit before you begin teaching it. The following is a sample letter that informs parents about the goals of the unit and introduces them to some of the activities their children will be doing.

Dear Parent,

In our next math unit, the class will investigate the ideas of probability. Students will do a variety of activities that involve them in making predictions, collecting data, using data to make decisions, and learning that some outcomes are more likely than others. Each activity also adds to the children's growing sense of numbers. They will compare numbers, do mental arithmetic, and practice addition and subtraction throughout the unit.

The class will also analyze games to decide if they are fair games or if one player has a better chance of winning than another. Playing games helps children develop thinking skills, proficiency with numbers, and a sense of sportsmanship. Keeping score, adding the numbers on two dice, and figuring how many more points one player has than others are all good ways for children to practice arithmetic while thinking about probability.

From time to time, your child's homework will be to teach a game we are investigating. We invite you to play the games with your child and talk with him or her about the underlying ideas.

Please come and visit us any time.

Sincerely,

A Final Comment

The decisions teachers make every day in the classroom are the heart of teaching. This book attempts to provide clear and detailed information about lessons and activities, organizing the classroom, grouping children, communicating with parents, and dealing with the needs of individual children. Keep in mind that there is no "best" or "right" way to teach the unit. The aim is for children to engage in mathematical investigations, be inspired to think and reason, and to enjoy learning.

CONTENTS

WHOLE CLASS LESSONS

The unit includes six whole class lessons, each requiring one to two class periods. Each lesson gives students a different way to think about probability.

In the first lesson, *Likely–Unlikely*, the children consider events in their lives that are likely and events that are unlikely. This lesson introduces vocabulary used throughout the unit, including *likely, unlikely, possible, impossible, certain, uncertain,* and *chance.*

The second lesson, *Empty the Bowl,* uses 1 die and a bowl with 12 tiles. The children roll the die, record the number that comes up, and take out that many tiles. They also keep track of how many rolls it takes to empty the bowl. The class gathers statistics and uses the data to determine how many rolls it typically takes to empty the bowl.

Is It 10? is a card game. Using decks of cards numbered from 1 (ace being 1) to 10, the children try to determine which is most likely—turning over two cards that are less than 10, equal to 10, or greater than 10.

Addition Facts and Strategies, the fourth whole class lesson, does not deal with probability but with addition facts. In most of the activities in this unit, children add numbers in the context of probability investigations. The activities provide natural springboards to having children explore strategies for the basic addition facts.

For *Spinner Experiment,* the fifth whole class lesson, students make spinners that are half red and half blue and use them for a probability experiment. The children predict what will happen, collect data in two different ways, look at their individual samples, and finally examine class results from the experiment.

In the sixth whole class lesson, *The Plus and Minus Game,* children determine whether or not a game is fair—that is, whether both players have an equal chance of winning. They write letters to a fictional game company to report their thinking. Then they try a new version of the game and again determine if it is fair.

WHOLE CLASS LESSON   Likely–Unlikely

Overview

The word *probability* and the concepts associated with this area of mathematics are, in most cases, new to first and second graders. This first lesson has two purposes: to introduce probability as a part of mathematics and to begin to explore the notions of probability that are part of students' everyday lives. The discussion and follow-up writing activity for this lesson provide opportunities for children to become familiar with some of the language they will use throughout the unit: *prediction, predict, chance, likely, unlikely, data, possible, impossible, certain, uncertain.*

The menu activity *Likely–Unlikely Book* (see page 94) extends this lesson by having students compile books of statements that describe likely and unlikely events in their lives. Also, the assessment *Likely and Unlikely* (see page 113) asks students to write individually about the meanings of these two words.

Before the lesson

Gather these materials:
- One sheet of chart paper, titled "Probability Words"
- Eight 4-by-18-inch tagboard strips. Write one of the following statements on each strip:

   Some babies will be born in the United States this week.
   It will rain here tomorrow.
   Everyone in our class will be sick on Friday.
   Someone will be absent this week.
   Only boys will be born in the United States this week.
   The principal will visit our class today.
   When you roll a die, you will get 1 six times in a row.
   The [use a popular local sports team] will win every game this season.

- Strips of 4-by-18-inch newsprint, two per pair of students
- Masking tape

Teaching directions

- Tell the children that they will begin a unit on probability. You may want to use this opportunity to review the other strands of mathematics.

- Post the sheet of chart paper titled "Probability Words."

- Initiate a class discussion about probability by talking with the children about weather and weather reporting. Ask questions such as:
   What information do you use to decide whether or not to take an umbrella (or wear a sweater or boots) to school?
   What words do weather reporters use to talk about the weather?
   What information does a weather reporter use to make predictions?

During the discussion, introduce probability terminology: *prediction, predict, chance, possible, probable, likely, unlikely,* and so on. As a word is mentioned, write it on the Probability Words chart.

■ Write the word *Likely* on the left side of the board and *Unlikely* on the right side. Show the strips of tagboard one at a time. Explain that the students will decide if each statement belongs in the likely or unlikely column. Read and sort the strips with the students.

■ Have the students return to their seats to work in pairs. Distribute a sheet of newsprint to each pair. Explain that they are to fold the paper in half, write *Likely* at the top of one half and *Unlikely* at the top of the other half.

Likely	UnLikely

■ Tell the children that they are to brainstorm events that are likely or unlikely. They should try to think of several ideas for each category and write at least one sentence for each. Tell them not to include the words *likely* or *unlikely* in their statements, so others can guess where they belong.

■ As the children finish their statements, give each pair two 4-by-18-inch strips of newsprint. Tell them to choose one statement from their likely list and one from their unlikely list and write each statement on a strip. Remind them to write large enough so that others can read the statements from across the room.

■ The next day, give the students time to finish writing their statements on strips. Then have them prepare to share their statements with the rest of the class. Tell pairs to choose one statement to read and decide who will hold the statement and who will read it. Give the children time to make their decisions and to practice reading.

■ Have partners come to the front of the room to read one of their statements. Let them call on someone to tell whether he or she thinks the statement is likely or unlikely. Have the children use masking tape to post their strips in the appropriate columns on the board. If time allows, have each pair read a second statement.

FROM THE CLASSROOM

NOTE It's important to foster a classroom environment where students listen to one another with respect. Establish a place in the room where the whole class can sit comfortably for the purpose of sharing their findings, discussing results, and watching activities modeled. Involve the children in developing guidelines so that all children can see and be heard.

NOTE It's helpful to compile a class chart of new terminology. Not only is the list useful for reinforcing vocabulary as it arises, but it is also a good reference for students as they write.

I began by calling one table at a time to come to the rug area. I asked the students to sit so that they could see the board comfortably. On some days this simple act takes longer than I would have imagined. On this day, Davy tried to sit between two people, where there was no room for another person. This caused an outcry, and I helped settle the children. Dean held back and couldn't seem to find a spot even after everyone else was seated. I suggested he pull up a chair and begin a balcony row. This idea caught on, and several others scrambled for chairs, eager for a balcony seat.

When the children were finally settled, I said, "Why don't we start out this way tomorrow? That way, we'll have rug sitters and back-row chair sitters. It gives us more space."

I then began to introduce the unit. "Today, we'll begin to learn about an area of mathematics we haven't studied yet this year," I said. "What are some of the areas of mathematics you know about?"

Several hands shot up.

Luisa said, "Multiplication."

"Measurement," Wade suggested.

"Fractions," Juliette added.

"Shapes have something to do with math," Kim offered.

"Does anyone know what part of mathematics has to do with looking at shapes?" I asked.

Kirk raised his hand and said tentatively, "Geometry?"

I agreed and went on to explain that besides geometry, measurement, and numbers, there are also patterns, logic, statistics, and probability. I pointed to the class chart that listed the different math strands. We had talked about the strands several times before, and I tried to review them on a regular basis.

"Today we will begin learning about the area of mathematics called *probability*," I said and pointed to the chart paper titled "Probability Words" that I had posted. I planned to use the chart for probability vocabulary introduced throughout the unit. "Has anyone heard the word *probability* before?" I asked.

"I heard it before," Mario said, "but I don't know what it is."

I explained that probability has something to do with making predictions and that we use probability in our lives every day to make decisions. I wrote *prediction* and *predict* on the Probability Words chart.

"Today when you left for school, some of you used probability to decide whether or not to bring an umbrella. Who brought an umbrella today?" I asked. A few hands went up.

"What information convinced you to bring an umbrella?" I asked.

Cecilia said, "My mother made me."

"Yeah," Chris moaned, "my mother always makes me."

Rachel added, "It's been raining for days."

"All you have to do is look out the window," Davy called out.

"How many of you have listened to a weather forecast on TV or on the radio?" I asked.

When several hands went up, I continued, "What kind of words do you hear weather reporters say when they predict the weather?"

I could tell that several children were frequent TV watchers. They sounded just like newscasters.

"There's an 80 percent chance of rain today," Nathan said. I wrote *chance* on the Probability Words chart.

"A slight chance of sprinkles tomorrow, clearing in the afternoon," added Lea.

"That's another way to talk about chance," I said.

"Rain most likely in the Bay Area," suggested Chris.

"Yes, sometimes rain is likely, and sometimes it's unlikely," I said, and wrote *likely* and *unlikely* on the chart.

"These are some of the words we'll be using when we talk about probability," I told them. "What information does a weather reporter use to make predictions about the weather?"

"They have satellite pictures," Nathan said.

"What else?" I asked.

"They have charts with temperature and things," added Natalya.

"Yes," I said. "They have lots of information and they use this data to help them make predictions. Collecting data will be an important part of our study of probability." I added the word *data* to the chart.

"Let's think about today at school and make some predictions. What are some things that are possible and some things that are impossible to happen today?" I asked, as I added the words *possible* and *impossible* to the Probability Words chart.

"It's possible that it will rain today," offered Luisa.

"It's impossible that a dragon will come into our classroom," Brian said with a giggle.

"It's possible the roof will leak today. It did in Mr. Mulkeen's class," Cindy said.

"It's impossible I will drive the car home today," Jack said.

I went on to say that there are some things we can be certain of and others that are uncertain. I added *certain* and *uncertain* to the Probability Words chart. I then asked, "Is it certain or uncertain that everyone will watch television tonight?" I called on Lea.

"Uncertain," she said.

"Why is it uncertain?" I asked.

Yasmine said, "Maybe someone's TV is broke."

I continued, "What about this statement: We will eat lunch today."

"Certain," several students called out.

"We better eat lunch every day," Mario chimed in.

Next, I wrote the word *Likely* on the left side of the board and *Unlikely* on the right side. I told the class that I had written some statements on strips of tagboard that we would read and decide whether they belonged in the Likely or Unlikely column.

I brought out the strips one at a time. We read each one and discussed whether the event was possible and, if possible, whether it was likely or unlikely to occur. There was some debate about whether it was possible for everyone to be absent on Friday.

"Everyone could get the chicken pox," Dean suggested, knowing why Aaron had been absent all week.

"That's impossible," Megan said. "I've already had the chicken pox." This created an outcry of "Me, too" from about half of the class.

NOTE All children, especially those who are new to English, learn vocabulary best when it's connected to experiences that are familiar to them.

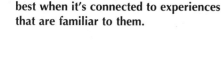

Not wanting to collect statistics on chicken pox, I went on to the other statements. After similar debates, the class decided to sort the statements in this way:

Likely
Some babies will be born in the United States this week.
It will rain here tomorrow.
Someone will be absent this week.

Unlikely
Everyone in our class will be sick on Friday.
Only boys will be born in the United States this week.
The principal will visit our class today.
When you roll a die, you will get 1 six times in a row.
The San Francisco Giants will win every game this season.

The statement that caused the most disagreement was the one predicting that the San Francisco Giants would win every game this season. Some loyal fans wanted it to be true. We wondered how many games a major league team played in one season and what a good record was for the whole season.

After this class discussion, I directed the students to return to their seats. When I had their attention, I said, "Together, you and your partner should think about events that are likely and unlikely. Think of a few things that are likely and a few that are unlikely. Then write at least one sentence for each.

"After everyone has done this assignment," I continued, "you'll share some of your statements with the class. Other students will try to decide whether your statement is likely or unlikely. This means you should not use the words *likely* or *unlikely* in your statements. When you've finished writing, raise your hand, and I'll come and tell you what to do next."

Before distributing the supplies, I demonstrated how the students' brainstorming papers should look. "Fold your paper in half and write *Likely* on one side and *Unlikely* on the other," I instructed as I made a sample. "Put both of your names on the paper."

Likely	UnLikely

I called on a few students to restate the directions in their own words to be sure they understood what they were to do.

"While I distribute the paper," I said, "talk to your partner about how you will work together."

Observing the Children

As I circulated, I looked to see who knew what to do and how the children worked together. I am continually amazed at how children attack tasks differently. Some seem to have no trouble getting started, and others seem to have no clue about what to do.

Fredric and Dylan wrote a humorous unlikely statement.

We will have recess every morning. [likely]
We will read a book today.

I will go to the corner store and buy 50,000 packs of bubble gum for 50¢ [unlikely]

By the time I had circulated around the room once, I could tell which pairs of students needed some assistance. I pulled my chair up to a table where Juliette was obviously troubled. She did not want to work with Dean. From past experience, she knew that he would not contribute and would make it difficult for her to do the activity by herself. I asked if either of them had an idea for the likely or unlikely list. They each had a suggestion, so I directed them to work together in a specific way. I explained that Juliette should write while Dean stated his idea, and then Dean should write while Juliette stated hers. I told them that I would return in a few minutes to see how they were doing. I hoped that if they became engaged in the activity, some of their antagonism would be tempered and they would be able to cooperate.

NOTE Working with a partner is not always easy, especially when writing is involved. Often one partner does all of the work, while the other turns off, gets bored, or is happy to let the partner do all the work. It's helpful to have successful partners share with the class their systems for working together. Remind students that they are responsible for making sure that both they and their partners contribute and participate fully. Frequent discussions about how to work with partners help children learn to work more cooperatively.

Dean and Juliette solved their difficulties working together by writing each other's statements.

likely	unlikely
Today we have recess.	someone saw a beanstalk.

As pairs of students finished and raised their hands, I gave them two 4-by-18-inch strips of newsprint and said, "Write a likely statement on one strip and an unlikely statement on the other. Later, you'll read one of your sentences to the class. Be sure to write large enough so students on the other side of the room can read your statements."

As with most assignments, a few students didn't finish. I collected the strips and told them that they would have time to complete their statements the next day.

A Class Discussion

Before class the next day, I again made two columns on the chalkboard with the headings *Likely* and *Unlikely*. I also prepared strips of masking tape so the children could tape their statements to the board. I then told the children what they would be doing.

"You and your partner will share one of your statements with the class," I said as I returned the large strips with the students' likely and unlikely statements. "If you haven't finished writing your sentences, you'll be able to do so in just a minute."

I explained that we would begin with each pair reading just one statement. "If there's time," I added, "you can read your second statement later. You both should agree on the statement you'll share and decide who will hold the strip and who will read it. After you read your statement, the class will try to decide if it's likely or unlikely."

I made sure to get around to all the pairs of students to see how they made their decision. Some asked if they could read two statements. I repeated the directions, reminding them that they could read only one. I told them that if there was time, we would read the others. I could tell that even though they had worked together on this task yesterday, some still felt ownership of "their" statements or "their" writing.

I gave the students five minutes to prepare. I took this time to help the few pairs who hadn't finished. Then I called for the children's attention. "I'll call one pair at a time to read a statement to the class," I said. "Partners will present a statement and then call on someone to tell whether the statement belongs under *Likely* or *Unlikely*."

The presentations went smoothly. I had to remind the students only once or twice to be good listeners. The children loved coming to the front of the room and enjoyed playing teacher when they called on another student. Many were careful not to call on someone who had already been called on.

To end the lesson, I called the students' attention to the Probability Words chart we had started the day before.

"What's the area of mathematics we're beginning to talk about?" I asked.

"Probability," several called out.

"Let's read the words we have on our list so far," I said.

We read aloud together: "Prediction, predict, chance, likely, unlikely, data, possible, impossible, certain, uncertain."

This is how the board looked after all the pairs had presented their statements:

Likely
We will read a book today.

The 49ers will beat the next team they are playing.

Someone likes to read.

Dogs are playful.

Brian's paper cut on his cheek will heal.

We will have homework tonight.

Someone in our class will have a birthday this month.

Unlikely
The President of the United States will teach us in room 204.

There will be an eclipse.

Someone saw a beanstalk.

We will have a fire drill today.

Children don't like to hear stories.

Children will draw on their table.

That it is going to snow.

This class will go to the zoo today.

WHOLE CLASS LESSON   Empty the Bowl

Overview

For this activity, each pair of students uses one die and a bowl of 12 Color Tiles. One partner rolls the die to determine how many tiles to remove from the bowl and then removes the tiles, while the other partner records the numbers rolled and keeps track of the number of rolls it takes to empty the bowl. Each pair plays the game at least five times, switching roles for each game and posting their results on a class chart. The class then discusses the likely number of rolls needed to empty the bowl. Playing this game helps develop number sense, as students record the numbers they roll and figure out how many tiles are left in the bowl.

The homework assignment *Empty the Bowl* (see page 164) asks students to teach the game to someone at home, play the game at least once, and then bring in the results. In the menu activity *Empty the Bowl with 20* (see page 75), students repeat this activity using 20 tiles, then compare the class results from the two experiments.

Before the lesson

Gather these materials:
- Small bowls (large enough to hold 12 Color Tiles), one per pair of students
- Color Tiles, 12 per pair of students
- Dice, one die per pair of students
- One sheet of chart paper, titled "Rolls to Empty the Bowl" and listing the numbers from 2 to 12 down the left side

Teaching directions

■ Explain how to play *Empty the Bowl.* Tell the students that they'll play this game in pairs, and each pair will need a bowl with 12 tiles, a die, and paper for recording. To play, they will roll the die, note the number that comes up, and take out that many tiles. While one person rolls the die and removes the tiles, the other will record each roll on a sheet of paper. They will continue rolling and removing tiles until the bowl is empty, and then they will record the number of rolls it took.

■ Choose a student to model the game with you. While one of you rolls the die and removes tiles, the other records on the board the numbers rolled and, when the bowl is empty, the number of rolls it took. Then trade jobs and play again. Modeling the game shows the children one way to cooperate when they play.

■ Explain that it's not necessary to go out exactly in this game. For example, if there are two tiles in the bowl, and a 5 comes up, it's okay to remove the two tiles and empty the bowl. Therefore, for some games, the total of the numbers rolled will be greater than 12.

■ Discuss with the class the fewest and the greatest number of rolls it could take to empty the bowl.

■ Post the chart titled "Rolls to Empty the Bowl." Show the students how to record on the class chart by making a tally mark to indicate the number of rolls it took to empty the bowl.

■ Have the students play *Empty the Bowl* at least five times. Remind them that for each game they must record the numbers they roll, count the number of rolls it took to empty the bowl, and record a tally mark on the class chart to indicate the number of rolls.

■ After all pairs have played at least five games, tell them to look at the results on their recording sheets. Initiate a class discussion, asking the students to share what happened when they played the game.

■ As a class, examine the class chart to identify the most and fewest number of rolls it took for anyone to empty the bowl. Ask the children to describe what else they notice about the data.

■ If you'd like, after the discussion have the children write a sentence describing something they noticed about the game. To help them get started, write a prompt on the board:

When you roll one die to empty the bowl,

_____ .

FROM THE CLASSROOM

I began class by saying, "Today you will learn a probability game that will also give you practice with addition. After you play the game for a while, we'll look at what's likely to happen." I pointed to the word *likely* on the Probability Words chart.

I wanted to get the students involved in the game quickly so that there would be time for them to play and then talk about their experiences. I had them gather around the rug near the board so I could demonstrate how to play.

"This game is called *Empty the Bowl,*" I told the class. "You'll play with a partner and for the two of you, you'll need a bowl, a die, 12 tiles, and paper."

I continued with the directions, "To play, one of you rolls the die and takes out that many tiles. Keep rolling and removing tiles until the bowl is empty. While one person rolls and removes tiles, the other person records on the paper."

I demonstrated the game to model how a student would take turns with a partner. I asked Cecilia to be my partner. Each time I rolled the die, I directed Cecilia to record on the board the numbers that came up. I asked the class how many tiles I had taken out of the bowl altogether and how many were left in the bowl. I kept the tiles I removed for each roll in a separate pile so that the children could see that the number of tiles for each roll matched the numbers that Cecilia wrote on the board. I told them that for this game it was okay not to go out exactly.

"If there are two tiles left in the bowl and you roll a 5," I explained, "you can take out the two tiles and record the 5."

After the bowl was empty, I asked Cecilia to write a plus sign between each of the numbers she had written. Then I directed the children to find the total for the numbers she had recorded: *2 + 6 + 2 + 5.* I gave several children a chance to report the total and explain their method. We all agreed that the total was 15. Cecilia recorded the total: *2 + 6 + 2 + 5 = 15.*

I asked the class, "How many rolls did it take to empty the bowl?"

Several students responded, "Four." I added another column to Cecilia's recording and labeled it: "Rolls."

$$2 + 6 + 2 + 5 = 15 \quad \overset{\text{Rolls}}{4}$$

Then I asked, "Why is the total 15, when I know there were only 12 tiles in the bowl when I started?"

I saw a few confused looks, but several children raised their hands to explain. I called on Nathan.

"It's because you rolled a 5 on the last roll," he said.

"What do you mean?" I asked.

"I mean, at the end, you had two tiles left but you rolled a 5. That means you had three extra," he explained.

"Did I go out evenly this time?" I asked, wanting to reinforce the fact that players didn't have to go out exactly.

A chorus of "no" followed.

"Sometimes your score will equal more than 12, and sometimes you will empty the bowl with exactly 12," I told the class.

I played another game with Cecilia. This time she rolled the die and removed the tiles, while I recorded. I wrote:

$$4 + 3 + 6 = 13 \quad \overset{\text{Rolls}}{3}$$

"What do you think is the fewest number of rolls it could take to empty the bowl?" I asked the class.

Several hands went up. I waited to give more children a chance to think about this problem. I repeated the question and asked them to talk to the students next to them to see if they had the same idea. While the children were talking to one another, several children called out, "Two."

After a few moments, I said, "It sounds as if many of you think that you could empty the bowl in two rolls. Who can explain one way to empty the bowl in two rolls?"

"You could roll two 6s," Kirk said.

"If you roll two 6s, would the bowl be empty?" I asked.

"Two 6s make 12, and there's only 12 tiles in the bowl," Jack said.

"Is there any other way to empty the bowl in two rolls?" I asked.

"No, because 6 is the highest number and it takes two 6s to make 12," Megan told us.

"You could use dice with bigger numbers," Rachel suggested.

"But with regular dice, the only way to empty the bowl in two rolls is to roll 6 twice," I said. Rachel nodded.

"What do you think is the most number of rolls it would take to empty the bowl with one regular die?" I asked.

"If you are really unlucky, you could roll all 1s," Chris said.

"It would take 12 1s," Natalya clarified.

I then directed the students' attention to the class chart I had posted on the front board. "When you and your partner have played *Empty the Bowl* five times," I said, "record the number of rolls it took for each round. When Cecilia and I played, it took four rolls for the first game, and three rolls for the second. We would put one tally mark next to the 4 and one tally mark next to the 3." I demonstrated by drawing tally marks on the class chart.

Rolls to Empty the Bowl	
2	
3	I
4	I
5	
6	
7	
8	
9	
10	
11	
12	

"After you and your partner finish five rounds," I continued, "you'll record five tally marks to show how many rolls it took for each of your games."

Before I dismissed the children to return to their seats, I asked them what their papers would look like for this activity. I knew that if I reviewed this with them, most would remember.

"You need to put two names on the paper," Jack volunteered.

"The title should be at the top," Juliette offered softly.

"What will the title be for this recording sheet?" I asked.

"Empty the Bowl," Chris said impatiently.

I told the children to play this game with someone at their table but with a different partner than they had worked with the day before. I suggested that one person from each side of the table switch seats just for this game. There was little resistance to this idea since the children were anxious to start playing.

The children returned to their seats. After a few adjustments for absentees, all were engaged in getting their papers ready and counting tiles into their bowls.

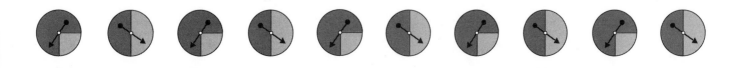

Observing the Children

As I circulated, I noticed that Rachel and Juliette were well into the activity. They had agreed that Juliette would do the writing and Rachel would roll the die and empty the bowl. On their third round, I stopped them. Juliette had recorded: *4 + 1 + 4.*

"How many tiles are out of the bowl so far?" I asked. I was curious to see if they could easily add the three numbers and tell how many were left in the bowl. Rachel quickly counted the tiles. Juliette, however, focused on the numbers on the recording sheet, counted aloud, "4, 5, 6, 7, 8, 9."

I called the girls' attention to the numbers and asked, "What is 4 plus 4?"

They both said, "Eight."

"What's 8 and 1 more?" I continued.

"Nine," they both responded.

I find that children often think that counting is the fastest and surest way to get the answer. They don't always make use of the written information in front of them. I constantly look for opportunities to help children gain confidence with what they already know about numbers.

"Okay," I said, covering the bowl, "if you know that nine tiles are out of the bowl, how many do you think are left in the bowl?"

They gave each other an oh-that's-easy look, each waiting for the other to say something. I waited. I knew they both were capable of figuring this out if they did the thinking that was necessary.

"Two—no, three," Juliette fumbled.

"Yeah, three," Rachel confirmed.

"How did you figure that out?" I asked Rachel.

"I know that 9 and 1 more makes 10. Since there's 12 in the bowl, you just need 2 more, I mean 3 more. Three more plus the nine," she managed to explain.

I moved on to make sure that everyone had been successful getting started and had found a way to work smoothly with his or her partner.

I noticed that Cindy and Yasmine were systematically taking turns with both the writing and the rolling of the die. I also noticed that they had forgotten to write the total after recording their rolls. I reminded them to do this, telling them that one of the things they were learning when they played this game was more about addition. I wanted the children to know that this was not just a fun game but a chance for them to practice their addition facts and investigate the ideas of probability.

When I came to Davy and his partner, I saw that the title on their paper had been erased. Davy was slowly rewriting it. Aaron was just sitting there looking a bit perturbed.

I asked, "Did you agree on who was going to do the writing for this game?"

Davy said, "Aaron just grabbed the paper and wrote our names and the title. So I erased it." Aaron kept quiet.

"It's usually best to talk about it before anyone starts writing. That way, things go more smoothly," I suggested. "Why don't you talk it over and make a decision about how you will share the writing? I'll get a new sheet of paper and come back to hear about your agreement."

In the rush and excitement to get started on something new, children often choose speed over negotiation. In the rush, some children seem to disregard their partners. Some partners allow this to happen. I constantly remind the children of the need to communicate with one another and work things out together.

When I returned with the paper, Davy told me that they had come to an agreement. I asked Aaron to tell me about it. He said, "We'll each write our own name."

"Then what?" I asked, wanting to hear more.

From the looks on their faces it was clear that they had gone no further in their thinking. I knew that unless they were in agreement about who would write the title and who would roll first, they would most likely have problems again. It would have been very easy for me to make the decision for them and hurry them along to play the game. But I felt that having them learn to make joint decisions was important and valuable.

"You need to find a way to decide who will write the title and who will write the numbers for the first round," I told them. "Discuss this with each other. I'll be back to hear what you decide."

As I checked on other partners, I noticed that Kirk and Fredric had two tiles left in their bowl. Kirk rolled a 4. Fredric recorded the 4 and put down the total as 14 without hesitating.

Cindy and Wade were across from them. They were about to empty their bowl. There were two tiles left, and Cindy rolled a 2. Wade recorded the 2 and proceeded to add up all of the numbers from the beginning. He had not thought to use the information he already had.

I returned to see how Davy and Aaron were doing. They were well into their second round, and I could tell they were taking turns with the writing. I didn't interrupt them but decided to talk to the whole class about working with partners before our next activity. We had talked about this many times, but it needed to be reinforced regularly.

NOTE Not all children find it easy to work together and share a task that involves exploring and recording. It's important to take the time to discuss with children how they might share the work in an assignment.

A Class Discussion

I stopped the students after most pairs had had a chance to play at least five rounds and record on the class chart. I had them put away their tiles and pencils so they could focus on their recording sheets. I asked them to look at the number of rolls it took to empty the bowl in each round and see what they noticed.

Juliette and Rachel said, "We got almost all four rolls."

Several pairs nodded in agreement.

Mario and Chris said, "We got mostly threes."

I asked if anyone had to roll more than four times to empty the bowl. Four hands went up.

Dylan reported, "Once it took us six rolls." Cindy and Yasmine reported that they also rolled six times.

"Let's look at the class chart," I said. "We can find out how many rolls it took for all the games you played."

The class results looked like this:

Rolls to Empty the Bowl

2	I
3	∦∦ ∦∦ ∦∦ ∦∦ ∦∦ ∦∦ I
4	∦∦ ∦∦ ∦∦ IIII
5	∦∦ ∦∦
6	IIII
7	
8	
9	
10	
11	
12	

NOTE *Data,* which I had introduced in the *Likely–Unlikely* lesson, was a new word for most of the children. However, rather than define or explain it, I referred to it in the context of the activity. Children learn vocabulary from seeing and hearing it used.

"What do you notice about our data for *Empty the Bowl?*" I asked.

"A lot of numbers got zero—7, 8, 9, 10, 11, 12," Matt remarked.

"Only one emptied the bowl in two rolls," Lea noticed.

"What did they roll?" I asked.

"Two 6s," several called out.

"What else do you notice?" I asked.

"There's 31 for 3," Mario said.

"Six rolls has only 4 tallies," Dylan added.

"There's 61 for 3," Timothy said, rather concerned and went up to the chart. He counted, "10, 20, 30, 40, 50, 60, 61."

"Those aren't 10s, those are 5s," Luisa corrected.

"Oh," said Timothy, realizing why he had been confused.

"Let's figure out how many there are for each number," I suggested. We counted by 5s for each set of tallies, and I wrote the total after each row. I also outlined the data.

Rolls to Empty the Bowl

2	I	1
3	∦∦ ∦∦ ∦∦ ∦∦ ∦∦ ∦∦ I	31
4	∦∦ ∦∦ ∦∦ IIII	19
5	∦∦ ∦∦	10
6	IIII	4
7		0
8		0
9		0
10		0
11		0
12		0

"Who can describe the shape that the data make?" I asked.

"It looks like a building on its side," Dean said.

"It's like stairs going down," Megan said.

"I think it looks like a finger pointing," Luisa said.

I asked the children to write a sentence that told something that was likely or unlikely to happen when they played *Empty the Bowl.* As a suggestion to help them get started, I wrote a prompt on the board:

When you roll one die to empty the bowl,

_____ .

The Children's Writing

Some students based their statements on their own experiences, not on the class data. For example, Matt and Randy played five games, all ending after four rolls. They wrote: *When we roll it all ways took 4 rolls to emtpey the bowl.*

For Matt and Randy, it always took four rolls to empty the bowl.

$$1 + 3 + 4 + 6 = 14 \quad | \quad \text{Rolls}$$
$$ \quad | \quad 4$$
$$6 + 5 + 1 + 3 = 15 \quad | \quad 4$$
$$6 + 3 + 3 + 2 = 14 \quad | \quad 4$$
$$3 + 3 + 4 + 6 = 16 \quad | \quad 4$$
$$2 + 2 + 2 + 6 = 12 \quad | \quad 4$$

When we roll it all ways took 4 rolls to empay the bowl.

Jack and Anne-Marie's small sample gave them the same information as the whole class data. They wrote: *It's likely to get 3 rolls. It's unlikely to get from 7 to 12 rolls.*

Jack and Anne-Marie predicted that it was likely to empty the bowl in three rolls.

Empty the Bowl (12)

1. 6 + 3 + 5 = 14   3 Rolls
2. 6 + 4 + 4 = 14   3
3. 3 + 6 + 5 = 14   3
4. 2 + 5 + 2 + 1 = 12   4
5. 6 + 3 + 2 + 6 = 17   4

It's likely to get 3 rolls.
It's unlikely to get from 7 to 12 rolls.

Adam and Anthony used the word *usually* as a synonym for *likely*. It was hard to tell from their statements whether they meant it was unlikely to get a 1 on the die or unlikely to empty the bowl in one roll. They wrote: *When you roll one die it is unlikely to get a one. It is usually to empty the bowl with three's roll.*

Carla and Timothy invented the word *unusually* to help them communicate their belief that it was unlikely to take 12 rolls to empty the bowl. The new word is actually a nice synonym for *unlikely,* and the awkwardness of their statement showed that the two children were willing to try integrating new terminology into their vocabulary. They wrote: *When you roll 1 die to empty the bowl You unusally to get roll the dice 12 times.*

Juliette and Lea based their statements on the class data, even though their own experience didn't match the larger sample. Although they rarely rolled 3 and only once emptied the bowl in three rolls, they wrote: *1. It is unlikly to get two. 2. It likly to get three.*

I gave the students the homework assignment *Empty the Bowl* (see page 164) and explained that when we started the menu, they would play *Empty the Bowl* again but with 20 tiles instead of 12.

Adam and Anthony used the word *usually* instead of *likely* in their second statement.

Empty the Bowl

Rolls

1. 5+2+5=12
2. 2+3+5+6=16
3. 3+4+6 = 13
4. 3+6+5=14
5. 6+2+5=13

3
3
3
3
3

When you roll one die it is unlikely to get a one. It is usually to empty the bowl with three's roll.

Juliette and Lea based their statements on the class data, not on their own games.

Empty the bowl

rolls

4+1+2+4+3=14   5
1+5+1+4+6=17   5
6+6=12   2
2+2+4+6=14   3
1+4+1+3+2=12   6

1. It is unlikly to get two.
2. It likly to get three.

Cindy and Holly attempted to explain why it usually took three rolls to empty the bowl.

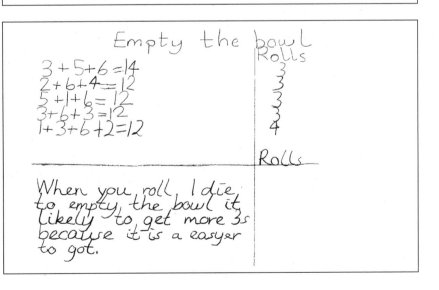

Empty the bowl

Rolls

3+5+6=14
2+6+4=12
5+1+6=12
3+6+3=12
1+3+6+2=12

3
3
3
3
4

Rolls

When you roll, 1 die to empty the bowl it likely to get more 3s because it is a easyer to get.

WHOLE CLASS LESSON   Is It 10?

Overview

In this lesson, students investigate whether the sum of the numbers on two playing cards chosen at random is likely to be less than 10, exactly 10, or greater than 10. Children play this game in pairs, using the ace through 10 cards from a standard deck of playing cards. To play, they each turn over a card, figure the sum of the two numbers, and record it as less than 10, exactly 10, or greater than 10. They record their totals on a class chart and later interpret the data to analyze what is likely and unlikely to happen when they play this game.

In the menu activity *Is It 12?* (see page 83), students play a similar game, then compare results from both games. Also, in the assessment *When You Turn Over Two Cards* (see page 89), students write about what is likely or unlikely to happen when they play *Is It 10?* and *Is It 12?*

Before the lesson

Gather these materials:
- ■ Playing cards, one deck per pair of students
- ■ One sheet of chart paper, titled "Is It 10?" and with three columns labeled "Less than 10," "Exactly 10," and "Greater than 10"

Is It 10?		
Less than 10	Exactly 10	Greater than 10

Teaching directions

■ If standard playing cards are new to the students, give them time to examine a full deck to become familiar with the cards. Encourage the children to sort and count the cards in different ways.

■ Tell the students that to play *Is It 10?* they need to use only the cards from ace to 10, and they should remove the face cards and jokers. Model this with a deck of cards. Explain that ace equals 1.

■ Model how to shuffle the cards by placing them face down on a table top and gently stirring them. Tell the children to shuffle the cards each time before dealing.

■ Choose two students to demonstrate the game while the rest of the class watches. Direct one of the students to deal the cards one at a time so that each player has 20 cards. Tell the students to keep their cards in a pile, face down.

■ Write three column headings on the board: "Less than 10," "Exactly 10," and "Greater than 10."

■ Tell the students demonstrating the game to turn over the top card on their piles. Have them say the two numbers and the sum. Record the sum in the appropriate column on the board. Have them repeat this.

$$\underline{\text{Less than 10}} \qquad \underline{\text{Exactly 10}} \qquad \underline{\text{Greater than 10}}$$
$$4 + 4 = 8 \qquad\qquad\qquad\qquad\qquad 6 + 5 = 11$$

■ Have the two students continue playing until they've turned over all of their cards. When the game is over, have the students count the number of combinations in each column and record the totals in the appropriate columns on the "Is It 10?" class chart.

■ Tell the class to play the game in pairs and record the sums on paper. Have the children play until all pairs have played at least one game.

■ Stop the class and ask the children to look at their papers. Ask volunteers to describe their data and tell what happened. Record their statements on the board. (This will be a useful introduction to their writing on the *Is It 12?* menu task.)

■ Have the students discuss the data on the class chart. Ask: What do you notice about the results on the class chart? What number do you see most often in each column?

FROM THE CLASSROOM

I began by asking the children to gather on the rug so I could show them a new activity. I noticed that the students were clearly getting better at forming a comfortable seating arrangement, although there were always a few who couldn't seem to find a spot without some help from me.

I told the class, "Today you will play a card game. You and your partner will look at two cards and add the numbers to decide if the sum is less than 10, exactly 10, or more than 10. You'll keep a record of your findings and later decide what is likely or unlikely to happen. This game is called *Is It 10?*"

I began sorting a deck of cards. "For this game you'll need a deck of cards without the face cards," I said. "What do I mean by face cards?"

Several hands went up, and I called on Megan.

"The jacks, queens, and kings," she said.

I removed the face cards. The deck I was using also had jokers, so I took them out and told the students that if their deck had jokers, they should also remove them. I then asked, "How many cards are there now?"

The usual hands shot up. I asked the students not to call out the answer and waited to give everyone a chance to think. I asked the question again,

and more hands went up this time. I want students to know that my questions are for everyone. I'm concerned that those who are not as quick as others will stop listening to questions if they know they won't have sufficient time to consider them.

I called on Aaron, who said, "There are 40."

"How do you know?" I asked.

"There's four 10s and that's 40," he answered.

I asked if others thought it was 40 and whether they had done it in a different way.

"I just went 10 plus 10 plus 10 plus 10 and got 40," said Cecilia.

"I said, 10, 20, 30, 40!" added Chris.

To bring the attention back to the game, I said, "For this game, you and your partner will share 40 cards equally. How many will each of you have?"

"I know that 20 and 20 makes 40," Yasmine offered.

I finished creating a deck with 40 cards and told the students that before they dealt the cards they should shuffle them.

"I know that some of you know how to shuffle cards," I said, "and I also know that when you try to shuffle in a fancy way, the cards can get bent. One way to shuffle so that the cards don't get bent is to stir them carefully like this." I modeled mixing the cards in a circular motion.

I asked Juliette and Matt to play the game while I kept score. I asked Juliette to deal the cards one by one so that she and Matt each had 20.

"Keep your cards in a pile, face down," I instructed. Then I wrote three column headers on the board:

Less than 10	Exactly 10	Greater than 10

I asked Juliette and Matt each to turn over his or her top card, say aloud the number on the card, figure the sum of the two numbers, and decide in which column the sum belonged. Juliette turned over an 8, Matt turned over a 5, and they said, "8 plus 5 is 13. That's more than 10." I wrote the number sentence in the greater-than-10 column.

After Juliette and Matt had played all their cards, the record on the board looked like this:

Less than 10	Exactly 10	Greater than 10
$4 + 2 = 6$	$5 + 5 = 10$	$8 + 5 = 13$
$4 + 1 = 5$		$9 + 2 = 11$
$1 + 2 = 3$		$10 + 1 = 11$
$2 + 3 = 5$		$8 + 3 = 11$
$4 + 3 = 7$		$10 + 6 = 16$
$4 + 1 = 5$		$7 + 5 = 12$
		$7 + 7 = 14$
		$6 + 10 = 16$
		$10 + 8 = 18$
		$9 + 8 = 17$
		$5 + 6 = 11$
		$8 + 3 = 11$
		$9 + 9 = 18$

"What do you notice about the results of the *Is It 10?* game?" I asked.

"They only got exactly 10 one time," Megan volunteered.

"What else?" I asked.

"They usually got greater than 10," added Fredric.

"How many times did the two cards equal a sum greater than 10?" I asked.

There was a murmur of counting, and several children called out 13. I wrote *13* under the column for greater than 10, *1* under the column for exactly 10, and *6* under the column for less than 10. Then I posted the chart paper titled "Is It 10?"

"When you finish a game, write the totals for each column on this class chart," I said as I wrote the numbers 6, 1, and 13 in the three columns.

Is It 10?		
Less than 10	Exactly 10	Greater than 10
6	1	13

"When you play your game, do you think you'll get the same results that Juliette and Matt did?" I asked.

"I think it is possible to get exactly 10 more than one time," Cecilia remarked.

"What makes you think that?" I asked.

"I don't know," she answered.

"You must have been thinking about something," I said, giving her another chance to think about it.

"There's other ways to get 10 besides 5 plus 5," she said.

"I don't think 10 will win because when you pick two cards you get mostly more than 10," Mario said.

Before the students returned to their seats to begin playing, I asked what they needed to write on their papers to prepare for the game. Each time students begin a new activity, I remind them to put their names and a title on their papers. I also remind children regularly to discuss who is going to write and how they can share the task. I find that things go more smoothly when I take time to talk with children about what they need to do to get started.

"If you have time, play two games with your partner," I said. "After you finish your first game, find the total for each column and write it on the class chart. We'll stop just before recess so that we can take a look at the results of our investigation."

Lea and Fredric correctly followed the directions for playing the game.

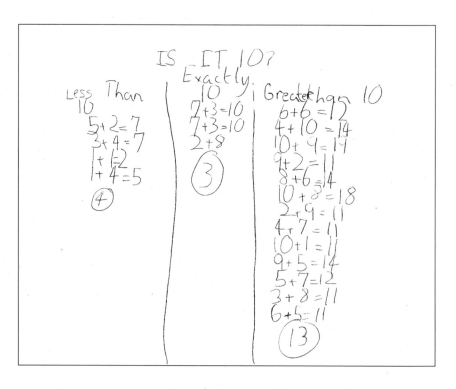

Like most students, Matt and Jack found that the greater-than-10 column had the most entries.

Observing the Children

The students began eagerly, as they seem to do with each new activity. As I went from table to table to see how they were doing, I was struck once again by the differences among children.

While Matt and Jack were taking turns writing their names and making the chart, Lea and Fredric were already well into playing the game. Davy and Luisa were still sorting cards.

As the children finished their games, they put their results on the class chart. For some this was a problem because writing on the class chart with a marker was seen as something special, and it took some negotiating for partners to agree on the division of labor.

A Class Discussion

I stopped the class with a little more than 10 minutes left in the period. Most of the pairs were on their second game, a few had just about finished their first game, and a few had started a third game. After I had everyone's attention and all pencils were down, I asked the children to study their papers with their partners.

"Talk to your partner about the data you recorded for this game," I said. "Try to think of a statement that tells what you think is likely or unlikely to happen when you play this game again."

Whenever I give directions for partners to talk to each other, I always find that there are a few children who don't seem to know what to do. I approach these pairs and gently help them begin interacting with each other. For example, I might ask, "What did you discover when you played this game?" After one child tells me something, I turn my attention to the other and suggest, "Now you tell your partner what you noticed."

After giving the students a few minutes to talk about their results, I had them share their findings. I wrote their statements on the board as they said them. I modeled writing statements because I knew that when the students repeated this activity in the menu activity (see page 83), they would be writing their own statements.

The students said the following about their results:

1. We usually get more than 10.
2. You don't get exactly 10 a lot.
3. We usually don't get 10.
4. We have too much more than 10.
5. On more than 10, we got 5 or more each time.
6. It's hard to get exactly 10.

I had hoped that the children would use the terms *likely* and *unlikely* when they offered their observations. When they didn't, I tried a different approach.

"After playing this game once or twice, you have some idea about what happens," I said. "Using your results and the statements on the board, talk to your partner about how you would finish these statements."

NOTE When teachers model writing while a child dictates, all children can see that the written descriptions come from their thinking and their words.

NOTE It's important to structure opportunities for children to use mathematical terminology. The more children hear and use new language, the more it will become part of their vocabulary.

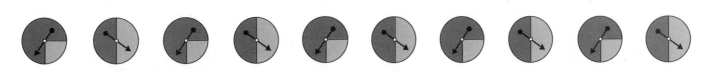

I wrote on the board:

When you play this game, you are likely _____ .
When you play this game, you are unlikely _____ .

I called on several students to present their ideas to the class.

Lea said, "When you play this game, you are likely to get more than 10 more."

Mitch added, "When you play this game, you are unlikely to get exactly 10 a lot."

Rachel said, "When you play this game, you are likely to get a few less than 10."

Jack said, "When you play this game, you are unlikely to get the same in each column."

I then said to the class, "You've looked at what happened when you played the game with a partner. Now let's look at the chart that shows what happened in all of your games."

Is It 10?

Less than 10	Exactly 10	Greater than 10
6	1	13
6	0	14
6	1	13
7	1	12
8	1	11
4	3	13
7	2	11
8	3	9
6	1	13
6	3	11
7	1	12
6	2	12
5	4	11
6	4	10
4	5	11

"What do you notice about the results on our class chart?" I asked.

"Most numbers are big in the greater-than-10 column," Luisa said.

"All the ones in less-than-10 are low numbers," Davy offered.

"Exactly 10 is low because it's rare to get exactly 10," Natalya said with authority.

"What number do you see most often in each column?" I asked. I gave the students time to examine the data and count.

"There's more 6s in the less-than-10 column," Fredric stated.

"Yeah, there's six 6s," Kim agreed.

"I think there are more 12s in the greater-than column," Lea offered.

"Exactly 10 has more 1s than other numbers," Mario said.

I told the children that on another day they would have a chance to play *Is It 12?* as a menu activity, and then we could see how the results compared.

A Note about the Probability

One way to look at the theoretical probability for *Is It 10?* is to examine an addition chart for the numbers 1 to 10. Out of 100 combinations, there are 36 ways to get a sum less than 10, 9 ways to get exactly 10, and 55 ways to get a sum greater than 10. The data that the children collected reflects a similar proportion. Although the thinking necessary to understand this idea is not accessible to first and second graders, their experience with playing the game, predicting, and looking at data provides valuable background for their later studies.

+	1	2	3	4	5	6	7	8	9	10
1	2	3	4	5	6	7	8	9	10	11
2	3	4	5	6	7	8	9	10	11	12
3	4	5	6	7	8	9	10	11	12	13
4	5	6	7	8	9	10	11	12	13	14
5	6	7	8	9	10	11	12	13	14	15
6	7	8	9	10	11	12	13	14	15	16
7	8	9	10	11	12	13	14	15	16	17
8	9	10	11	12	13	14	15	16	17	18
9	10	11	12	13	14	15	16	17	18	19
10	11	12	13	14	15	16	17	18	19	20

WHOLE CLASS LESSON

Addition Facts and Strategies

Overview

NOTE The NCTM's *Curriculum and Evaluation Standards for School Mathematics* states on page 47: "Children should master the basic facts of arithmetic that are essential components of fluency with paper-and-pencil and mental computation and with estimation. At the same time, however, mastery should not be expected too soon. Children will need many exploratory experiences and the time to identify relationships among numbers and efficient thinking strategies to derive the answers to unknown facts from known facts."

Many children at this age are successful in finding the answer to basic addition problems by counting. Although counting is a legitimate strategy, this lesson asks students to think of other ways to figure sums.

This lesson doesn't relate directly to students' study of probability, but it's timely to include in this unit for several reasons. Many of the activities in the unit require the children to add, and competency with addition enhances children's access to the activities and helps them focus on the probability ideas. Also, when students have the chance to hear a variety of strategies for adding, they can learn different ways to think about finding sums.

The lesson has two parts. In Part 1, students examine the 121 addition facts and talk about which ones are easy. They also explain some ways to figure out difficult facts. In Part 2, students again offer strategies for figuring out the addition facts they don't "just know." This time, the teacher writes their ideas on the board.

In the related assessment *Strategies for 7 + 6* (see page 65), each student writes three strategies for solving the sum 7 + 6.

Before the lesson

Gather these materials:
■ A chart of addition facts as shown, written on the board or on a large chart. You can also write the number facts on cards and arrange them in a large pocket chart.

0 + 0	1 + 0	2 + 0	3 + 0	4 + 0	5 + 0	6 + 0	7 + 0	8 + 0	9 + 0	10 + 0
0 + 1	1 + 1	2 + 1	3 + 1	4 + 1	5 + 1	6 + 1	7 + 1	8 + 1	9 + 1	10 + 1
0 + 2	1 + 2	2 + 2	3 + 2	4 + 2	5 + 2	6 + 2	7 + 2	8 + 2	9 + 2	10 + 2
0 + 3	1 + 3	2 + 3	3 + 3	4 + 3	5 + 3	6 + 3	7 + 3	8 + 3	9 + 3	10 + 3
0 + 4	1 + 4	2 + 4	3 + 4	4 + 4	5 + 4	6 + 4	7 + 4	8 + 4	9 + 4	10 + 4
0 + 5	1 + 5	2 + 5	3 + 5	4 + 5	5 + 5	6 + 5	7 + 5	8 + 5	9 + 5	10 + 5
0 + 6	1 + 6	2 + 6	3 + 6	4 + 6	5 + 6	6 + 6	7 + 6	8 + 6	9 + 6	10 + 6
0 + 7	1 + 7	2 + 7	3 + 7	4 + 7	5 + 7	6 + 7	7 + 7	8 + 7	9 + 7	10 + 7
0 + 8	1 + 8	2 + 8	3 + 8	4 + 8	5 + 8	6 + 8	7 + 8	8 + 8	9 + 8	10 + 8
0 + 9	1 + 9	2 + 9	3 + 9	4 + 9	5 + 9	6 + 9	7 + 9	8 + 9	9 + 9	10 + 9
0 + 10	1 + 10	2 + 10	3 + 10	4 + 10	5 + 10	6 + 10	7 + 10	8 + 10	9 + 10	10 + 10

Part 1: Examining the Addition Chart

■ Discuss the different basic addition facts students need to know to play the games *Empty the Bowl* and *Is It 10?*

■ Display the chart of addition facts from 0 + 0 to 10 + 10. Ask the children how many facts they think are on the chart, and then tell them there are 121. Ask volunteers to describe patterns they notice on the chart.

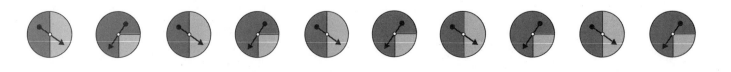

■ Have the children look at the 121 addition facts and talk about which ones they already know. (Typically, children name adding 0 and 1.) Delete these facts by erasing them, crossing them out, or removing them from the pocket chart. (Some children might volunteer that they know other facts, but delete only those that all of the children know.)

■ Write *7 + 6* on the board and have children describe how they would figure out the answer. Record their methods on the board. It may help to prompt students by asking them to tell how they would help a younger child solve this problem.

■ Write *6 + 3* on the board. Explain that if you know the sum for this fact, you automatically know another. Ask the children if they can tell you the other one. If no child identifies 3 + 6, then write it on the board and explain that the two sums are the same with the numbers reversed. If you like, introduce the terminology *commutative pairs.*

■ Have the children find on the chart pairs of facts with reversed addends—3 + 6 and 6 + 3, 7 + 4 and 4 + 7, and so on. Erase, cross out, or remove one of each pair. (Note: Typically children prefer to add facts with the larger addend first, as it's quicker to find the sum by counting on. To respond to this and to be consistent, eliminate all those with the smaller addend first.)

Part 2: Strategies for Adding

■ Have students review how you removed combinations from the addition chart.

■ Tell students that they will again figure out the sum for a harder addition fact and share their strategies.

■ Record students' strategies on the board to model how to put their thinking into writing.

FROM THE CLASSROOM

Part 1: Examining the Addition Chart

I asked the students to recall the two games we had learned over the past week. I wrote the names of the games on the board: *Empty the Bowl* and *Is It 10?* I asked what they thought they were learning while they played these games. I wanted the children to be aware that the games they were playing had several mathematical purposes.

"We're doing math," said Kim.

"We're solving problems," added Natalya.

I agreed with these ideas and continued to probe, "What else are you learning?"

Mario's hand shot up, "We're doing likely and unlikely."

I nodded and asked, "What part of mathematics deals with looking at what's likely and not likely?" Several children looked over at the Probability Words chart and called out, "Probability!" I agreed that we were indeed working with probability ideas. I asked again, "What else are you learning?"

"We're learning addition," said Kirk.

I used Kirk's comment to begin talking about the addition facts. (If no child had mentioned addition, I would have pointed out to the class that they used addition in both games.)

I directed the students to the chart of addition facts. "All the basic addition facts from zero plus zero to 10 plus 10 are listed on the back board," I said. "How many addition facts do you think are on the chart?" After looking at the chart, many children estimated 100. I told them that there were 121.

I then had the students gather around the board so we could focus on the chart more closely. I told them that there were a lot of facts to know but I thought that they already knew many of them. To help them become familiar with the chart, I asked them to describe any patterns they saw. Lea noticed that for each column, the second number was the same across each row. "They go zero, 1, 2, 3, 4, 5, 6, 7, 8, 9, 10," she said.

Dylan saw that the first number in each combination stayed the same for the entire column: The first number in the first column was always 0; in the next column, it was always 1; and so on.

Timothy found the doubles in the diagonal: 0 + 0, 1 + 1, 2 + 2, etc. I circled the doubles as he read them.

Then Cecilia told us that all the numbers in the other diagonal equaled 10. There was a murmur of agreement, as others realized that she was adding the two numbers in each combination.

"Let's talk about the number facts you already know. Which ones are the easiest?" I asked.

Luisa said, "It's easy to add zero."

"Why is it so easy?" I asked her.

She said, "It's like adding nothing. You just get the same number."

I erased the zero row and zero column. (If I had written the facts on chart paper, I would have crossed out the zero row and zero column.)

"The 1s are pretty easy, too," Yasmine piped in. "You just get the next number."

I asked if someone had another way to explain why adding 1 was so easy.

Rachel said, "It's like counting on 1 more."

I erased the 1s row and 1s column.

2 + 2	3 + 2	4 + 2	5 + 2	6 + 2	7 + 2	8 + 2	9 + 2	10 + 2
2 + 3	3 + 3	4 + 3	5 + 3	6 + 3	7 + 3	8 + 3	9 + 3	10 + 3
2 + 4	3 + 4	4 + 4	5 + 4	6 + 4	7 + 4	8 + 4	9 + 4	10 + 4
2 + 5	3 + 5	4 + 5	5 + 5	6 + 5	7 + 5	8 + 5	9 + 5	10 + 5
2 + 6	3 + 6	4 + 6	5 + 6	6 + 6	7 + 6	8 + 6	9 + 6	10 + 6
2 + 7	3 + 7	4 + 7	5 + 7	6 + 7	7 + 7	8 + 7	9 + 7	10 + 7
2 + 8	3 + 8	4 + 8	5 + 8	6 + 8	7 + 8	8 + 8	9 + 8	10 + 8
2 + 9	3 + 9	4 + 9	5 + 9	6 + 9	7 + 9	8 + 9	9 + 9	10 + 9
2 + 10	3 + 10	4 + 10	5 + 10	6 + 10	7 + 10	8 + 10	9 + 10	10 + 10

I told the children that while they "just know" some facts, they need strategies to help them figure out other facts. I wrote on the board:

$$7 + 6$$

"If you don't just know this one, how can you figure it out?" I asked.
Wade said, "If you know 6 plus 6, it's just 1 more."
Megan said, "Or you could do 7 plus 7 and 1 less."
I wrote on the board:

Start with doubles.

Mario had a different approach to suggest. He said, "You could go 7, 8, 9, 10, 11, 12, 13," demonstrating his method for the class by counting on his fingers to keep track.
"That's the way I do it," Natalya commented.
I wrote *Count on* beneath *Start with doubles* and then asked, "Does anyone have another strategy for figuring out how much 7 plus 6 is?" I called on Chris.
"You can take 3 from the 6," he said, "and put it on the 7 to get 10. Then 3 more makes 13." I added Chris's suggestion to the list. The final list looked like this:

Start with doubles.
Count on.
Make a 10.

I pursued one more point about the combinations on the chart, taking the opportunity to talk with the children about the commutative property of addition. I wrote on the board the addition fact *6 + 3* and asked, "If you know this one, what other one do you automatically know?"
Several students answered, "3 plus 6."
"Which one is easier to learn?" I asked.
Nathan said, "It's easier to do 6 plus 3 because if you started with 6 you would only need to count on 3."
I then said, "Number combinations like 3 plus 6 and 6 plus 3 are called commutative pairs. Can you say 'commutative pairs'? Try it together softly." The children all tried saying the phrase.
I wrote two more facts on the board: 8 + 5 and 5 + 8. "These are also commutative pairs," I said. "Which one is easier to figure out?"
Cecilia said, "I think 8 plus 5 because it's easier to start with the big number."
I then had them look for commutative pairs on the chart. We found 6 + 3 and then 3 + 6, 8 + 5 and 5 + 8, 9 + 7 and 7 + 9. Each time, I erased the fact with the smaller addend first. Soon it was becoming obvious that the bottom left side of the chart (below the doubles diagonal) could be eliminated.
Finally, I had erased the bottom left-hand side of the chart. As I did this, Natalya said, "You mean you wrote all those numbers for nothing?"
"I guess I did," I replied. The chart looked like this:

2 + 2	3 + 2	4 + 2	5 + 2	6 + 2	7 + 2	8 + 2	9 + 2	10 + 2
	3 + 3	4 + 3	5 + 3	6 + 3	7 + 3	8 + 3	9 + 3	10 + 3
		4 + 4	5 + 4	6 + 4	7 + 4	8 + 4	9 + 4	10 + 4
			5 + 5	6 + 5	7 + 5	8 + 5	9 + 5	10 + 5
				6 + 6	7 + 6	8 + 6	9 + 6	10 + 6
					7 + 7	8 + 7	9 + 7	10 + 7
						8 + 8	9 + 8	10 + 8
							9 + 9	10 + 9
								10 + 10

NOTE Students need to know that they are expected to communicate about mathematical ideas and that classroom discussions contribute to the growth of these ideas. As teachers, we should help children get used to paying attention to one another's ideas. We also need to decide how long a group can benefit from sharing and listening to any one group discussion.

There were 45 facts left for the children to learn. The list looked more manageable, but there was still a lot for the children to learn and remember.

We had been talking for a while now, and I ended the conversation. There was more I wanted to discuss, but I decided not to push for more now. I planned to take time for these kinds of discussions regularly throughout the unit.

Part 2: Strategies for Adding

I began class the next day by reminding the students that we had looked at the chart of addition facts and they had shared their strategies for figuring out 7 + 6.

The day before had been the children's first opportunity to explain how they figured out addition facts they didn't "just know." I had kept the focus on communicating orally and on trying a variety of approaches. Today I planned to model how to write about strategies. The discussion would provide another chance for those students who didn't yet have strategies to hear how other students approached adding. Also, for a later assessment, I planned to ask the students to write individually about how they would find the sum for a specific addition fact. (See page 65.)

"I want you each to figure out the sum of 8 plus 7," I said as I wrote 8 + 7 on the board. "In a moment, you'll share your strategies, and I'll write what you say on the board. Don't call out or raise your hand yet. I want everyone to have a chance to think about the problem." I know that once a child has an answer, the need to blurt it out is almost uncontrollable. This robs the other children of their chance to think.

After a few moments, I called on Brian.

"I counted," he said.

I asked Brian to explain exactly how he counted. He modeled with his fingers how he started at 8 and counted on 7 more with his fingers until he got to 15. I wrote on the board:

1. Start at 8 and count 7 more with your fingers.

Fredric reported, "I did 7 plus 7 then plus 1 equals 15."
"Why did you add 7 plus 7?" I asked him.
"Because it's easy; it's a double," he answered. I wrote on the board:

2. Add 7 + 7 because it's a double. Then add 1 to make 15.

Luisa was anxious to share her method. She had difficulty explaining what she did and started to get lost in her effort to put it into words. English is not Luisa's first language.

She began, "I just minus 2 from 7. Then there was 5. I add a 1 and . . . get 15."

I asked Luisa why she added a 1. She wasn't sure. I reviewed what she had said. "You took 2 from the 7 and got 5." Luisa nodded. "What did you do with the 2?" Luisa still looked a little lost.

Juliette said, "I think she did the 'make a 10' method."

I asked Luisa if that's what she needed the 2 for. She looked relieved and said yes. I wrote on the board:

3. Make a 10.
   7 − 2 = 5
   8 + 2 = 10
   10 + 5 = 15

I explained, pointing to what I had written, "Take 2 from 7 and get 5. Put the 2 with the 8 to make 10, then add the 5 to get 15. This is the 'make a 10' method."

Timothy raised his hand and said that he had another way. "I know 10 plus 10 is 20. So I just take 5 away from 20 and it's 15," he said.

I saw that Timothy had found a way to use the "double a number" method to get to 15. However, I also saw that he had lost the connection to the original problem and was now finding a way to make 15. I asked Timothy how the 10 + 10 related to the original problem of 8 + 7. He looked perplexed; he had not used 8 + 7 in his problem. I assured him that his method was a way to find 15, but our problem was how to do 8 + 7.

Holly said, "I know that 7 plus 7 equals 14. If you add an 8 it's one number higher."

"Holly's method sounds like Fredric's," I said. Several children nodded. "I'll write it anyway," I added, "because even though it's similar, Holly's words are different."

4. 7 + 7 = 14. If you add an 8 it's one number higher.

Chris told us his method: "I did 8 plus 8 is 16, take away 1 is 15."
I recorded:

5. 8 + 8 is 16, take away 1 is 15.

When it appeared that no one had another method to offer, I had the children choose menu activities to work on for the remainder of the period.

WHOLE CLASS LESSON ■ Spinner Experiment

Overview

In this lesson, children learn how to construct a spinner. They predict what will happen when they spin many times. They spin, record, and then combine their individual results into a larger class sample.

Through this activity, children experience what can happen when two events are equally likely to occur. They also examine the difference between the small samples of data from their individual experiments and a larger sample from the entire class. The children are learning about making predictions, collecting data, and interpreting results.

The menu activity *More Spinners* (see page 117) repeats this investigation using a different spinner. In the assessment *100 Spins* (see page 127), students predict what would happen if they spun the second spinner 100 times. They get a chance to test their predictions after doing the homework assignment *Spinners* (see page 165).

Before the lesson

Gather these materials:
■ One spinner made following the directions below
■ How to Make a Spinner, copies for students and one copy enlarged and posted (See Blackline Masters section, page 175.)
■ Spinner Faces #1, cut in quarters so that each student gets one face (See Blackline Masters section, page 176.) (Use a compass point to poke a hole in the center of each spinner face.)
■ 5-by-8-inch index cards, one per pair of students (Cut each one in half so each student gets a 5-by-4-inch card. Use a compass point to poke a hole near the center of each piece.)
■ Paper clips, one per student (Pull up one end of each paper clip so that it is perpendicular to the rest of the paper clip.)

■ Plastic straws, one ¼-inch length per child
■ Scissors
■ Tape
■ Snap (or other interlocking) cubes, 10 red and 10 blue for each pair of students, plus 10 more of each for modeling the lesson
■ Spinner recording charts, cut so that each pair of students gets one recording chart (See Blackline Masters section, page 178.)

Teaching directions

■ Show the students the spinner you made. Spin the spinner and point out how the indicator line tells what color the spinner lands on. Tell the children that they will work in pairs, but they'll each make their own spinner.

■ Model for the class how to make a spinner.

1. Color a spinner face half red and half blue.
2. Cut out the spinner face.
3. On the card, draw a line from the hole in the middle to one corner.

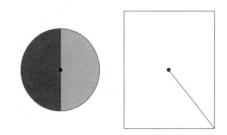

4. Write your name on the other side of the card.
5. Push the bent end of the paper clip through the hole in the index card. Tape the rest of the paper clip to the bottom of the card. Make sure the side of the card with the line is facing up.

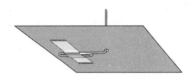

6. Put the piece of plastic straw and then the spinner face on the paper clip.

7. Cover the tip of the paper clip with a piece of tape.

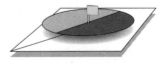

■ Have the children predict what will happen when you spin this spinner many times.

■ Gather 10 red and 10 blue cubes. Ask two students to use the spinner you made to demonstrate the *Spinner Experiment.* Have one student spin the spinner and the other be the recorder. Each time the spinner lands on a color, the recorder takes a cube of that color, snapping together cubes of the same color. The students stop when they use up all the cubes of one color. Demonstrate how to use red and blue crayons or marking pens to record results on the recording chart. Then have the students place the two stacks of cubes on the chalkboard tray. Remind students that each pair should keep their two stacks together on the tray.

■ List on the board the directions the class is to follow:

1. Make a spinner.
2. Spin the spinner with a partner.
3. Keep track of your spins using cubes. Stop when you have 10 of one color.
4. Color in your recording chart to show your results.
5. Place your red and blue stacks on the chalkboard tray.

■ Explain that even though pairs need only one spinner, each student should make one so they all will have their own later.

■ Ask several students to help you distribute the supplies needed for making the spinners. Have students make their spinners and then do the experiment. Encourage students who finish early to help other students or repeat the experiment without using the red and blue cubes, but just coloring on a recording chart.

■ When all students have completed the experiment and placed their stacks of cubes on the chalkboard tray, gather the class. Ask the children to predict how the trains will compare if all the red cubes are snapped together into one train and the blue cubes into another.

■ Have children snap together the stacks and compare them. Discuss the difference between the class results and individual results.

■ Tell the students to attach their recording charts to a piece of lined paper and write about the experiment. To help the children get started, write a prompt on the board:

We made a spinner that is half red and half blue. We spun it many times and _____.

FROM THE CLASSROOM

I gathered the spinner I had made and all of the materials needed to make the spinners and asked the children to come to the front of the room so they could see what I was doing. I told them that they would make spinners to use for a probability experiment. I demonstrated as I gave directions.

"You'll work with a partner, but each of you will make your own spin-ner," I explained as I held up the spinner I had made earlier. I demon-strated how to spin the spinner, showing how the line indicated what color the spinner landed on.

"What if it lands on a line?" Chris asked.

"I know," Natalya said. "You do it over."

Then I held up a spinner face. "Listen to my directions carefully and watch what I do," I told the children. "First, you need to color your spinner face. If you color it before you cut it out, then you don't have to be so careful about staying inside the lines when you color." I colored a spinner face half red and half blue.

"When you've colored the spinner face, cut it out carefully," I said, and demonstrated.

"Next, draw a line on the card from the hole in the center to one cor-ner. This line will be the spinner pointer," I said. I used a ruler to show them where the line should go.

"Be sure to write your name on the other side of the card, so you'll always be able to find your spinner," I added, turning over the card and writing my name on the back.

"Put your spinner together in this way: The point of the paper clip goes through the hole in the bottom of the square base. Tape the rest of the clip to the back of the card so that it doesn't slip out." As I gave these direc-tions, I modeled for the children what they were to do.

"Next, put the small piece of plastic straw on the paper clip point, and then put the spinner face on top of the straw," I continued. "Finally, put a small piece of tape on the point of the paper clip, like this." I wrapped the tape around the point.

"Can we take ours home?" several students asked.

"You'll use your spinner for an experiment today. In a few days, you may take your spinner home. You can also try making one on your own some time," I said.

The children were anxious to make their spinners. However, I wanted to pose a problem and talk about it before they returned to their seats.

"Who can describe this spinner?" I asked holding up the one that was half blue and half red.

"It's a 50-50 chance," Fredric offered.

"Who can explain what Fredric means by 50-50?" I asked, writing *50-50 chance* on the Probability Words chart.

"It means like equal," Cindy explained.

"Blue and red are the same," Jack added.

"When people work on probability experiments, they try to predict or guess first what will happen," I said, pointing to *predict* on the Probability Words chart. "If we spin this spinner many times, what do you predict will happen?"

"I think blue will win," Dylan called out.

"What makes you think that?" I asked.

"I just do," Dylan replied, shrugging his shoulders.

"Red might win," Aquilina said.

"Why do you think red?" I asked.

"Well, maybe it will be a tie," she said, changing her mind. "You can't really tell."

"I think blue," Lea said. "If you get blue first and go blue, red, blue, red, blue would win."

"You can't be sure," Dean responded.

"You all have different ideas. We'll have to spin and find out," I said. "When you do this experiment, you'll collect data in two ways. Each time you spin, you take a cube for the color that comes up. If your spinner lands on red, take a red cube; if it lands on blue, take a blue cube. You'll start with 10 cubes of each color. When you use up all the cubes of one color, stop."

So that all of the children would know exactly what to do when they returned to their seats, I decided to have two students model how to spin and use the cubes to keep track. I asked Anthony and Lea to come up and demonstrate. I asked Lea to spin and Anthony to record by snapping together the cubes. After Lea had spun seven times, I suggested that Anthony spin while Lea snapped the cubes. When they finished, they had a stack of 10 red cubes and a stack of 7 blue cubes. I told them to place the stacks on the chalkboard tray.

"When you finish your experiment, you should put your stacks of cubes on the chalkboard tray, as Lea and Anthony did," I said. "Then record the results on this recording chart." I held up a sample of the chart the children were to use.

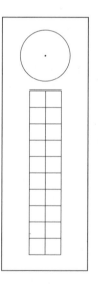

"What do you think I should put on this blank circle?" I asked, pointing to the circle at the top of the recording chart.

"I think you draw a picture of the spinner," Aquilina offered.

"Yes," I said. "Then show how many reds and how many blues you got by coloring the squares. How many reds will I color to show what Lea and Anthony spun?"

"You should color 10 reds and 7 blues," Aaron said. I colored the recording chart.

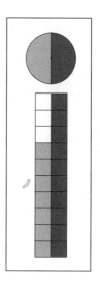

I asked three students to help distribute the materials. Also, since I had given so many directions at one time, I decided to list them on the board before the children began to work:

1. Make a spinner.
2. Spin the spinner with a partner.
3. Keep track of your spins using cubes. Stop when you have 10 of one color.
4. Color in your recording chart to show your results.
5. Place your red and blue stacks on the chalkboard tray.

Observing the Children

The children quickly went to work making their spinners. Most had no trouble at all. The paper clip caused a few problems when some children tried to open it farther or put it in from the top instead of from the bottom of the spinner. Overall, I was impressed with the students' ability to make the spinners.

When the children had made their spinners, they were thrilled to see how they worked. Many students wanted to show me how successful they had been, and they brought their spinners to me to demonstrate how well they spun.

"Now that you've made your spinner, what do you do next?" I asked the children, encouraging them to check the directions on the board.

"We spin and keep track with cubes," Yasmine said quickly going back to her seat to talk to her partner.

"Oh, yeah," Matt said, remembering what to do next.

Soon everyone was spinning and building stacks with their cubes to show the results of their experiment. As pairs finished, I reminded them to place their cubes on the chalkboard tray next to Lea and Anthony's.

"Be sure to keep your blue and red stacks next to each other. We want to see the results from each pair," I said.

"Can we do it again?" Cindy asked.

"We don't have enough cubes for everyone to do it again," I answered, "but if you have enough time, you may do it without the cubes, just by coloring in another recording chart."

A Class Discussion

When most of the students had done the experiment once, I asked that all the children sit on the rug by the board, so we could look at our data.

"What do you notice about the results?" I asked. Several children had been busy counting and organizing the trains while they were waiting for others to complete the experiment. They had anticipated the question and were prepared to answer.

"Blue won eight times," Aquilina reported.

"Red only won six times," Nathan told us.

I asked Brian to point to the pairs of cubes that showed blue was the winner.

"What do you predict will happen if we snap all the red cubes together and all the blue cubes together into two long trains?" I asked.

"I think blue will win," Juliette said.

"Probably blue," Wade added.

I chose two students to snap the red cubes together and two others to snap the blue cubes together. There was great anticipation. The students were surprised when we found that the blue train had only four cubes more than the red train.

"What do you think would happen if we did this again tomorrow?" I asked.

"Maybe red would win," Chris said.

"I think blue," Lea said.

Some children wanted to count the cubes in each long train. I suggested they do this later. "We're going to write about the spinner experiment now," I said.

I asked the children to return to their seats and had monitors collect the unused cubes. Once everyone was settled, I gave directions.

"First, tape your recording chart to a sheet of lined paper," I told them. "Then write about what happened when you spun your spinner."

I wrote this prompt on the board for those who needed it:

> We made a spinner that is half red and half blue. We spun it many times and
>
> _____.

As the children were busy writing, I collected the spinners and put them in a box, so the children could take them home later.

The Children's Writing

Most of the children used the prompt I had written on the board and then recorded only what color "won." For example, Juliette and Bart wrote: *We made a spinner it is half red and half blue. We spun it many times and red won.*

Juliette and Bart explained how red won the game.

Spinner Experiment

We made a spinner it is half red and half blue we span it many times and red won. This is are data red has ten and blue has five.

Some students took one color as his or her own. For example, Randy chose red and Aaron chose blue. Randy was elated when he "won." He wrote: *We made a spinner. it is half red and half blue. We spun it many times and <u>red</u> won. The skore was 10 to 5. It was very fun! I won I was red.*

Anthony didn't use my prompt but wrote his own analysis of the activity: *blue had one more block then red. we roled the spiner and blue got it first. We spun the spiner and <u>blue</u> won.*

(left) Randy wanted red to win and was excited when it did.

(right) Anthony explained what happened in his experiment.

Spinner Experiment

We made a spinner it is half red and half blue. We spun it many times and <u>red</u> won. The skore was 10 to 5. It was very fun! I won i was red.

Spiner Exsperiment

blue had one more block then red. we roled the spiner and blue got it first.

We spun the spiner and <u>blue</u> won.

WHOLE CLASS LESSON   The Plus and Minus Game

Overview

This activity puts pairs of students into an imaginary situation where they research a new game for a toy company. Their job is to test the game, decide if they would recommend it, and write a letter to the company about their findings. The next day, they test a different version of the same game.

In the related menu activity *The 1 to 10 Game* (see page 148), students develop strategies for playing a game that was invented by two second graders. Also, in the menu activity *Invent a Game* (see page 153), students invent their own games and discuss what makes a good game.

Before the lesson

Gather these materials:
■ Dice, two per pair of students

Teaching directions

Part 1: Playing the Game

■ Begin by talking to the class about how game manufacturers get their ideas for new games. Explain that a company tests each new game to decide whether or not it's good. Tell the students that you have a new game for them to test.

■ Present the rules for *The Plus and Minus Game:* Players decide who will be Player 1 and who will be Player 2. Each person rolls a die at the same time. If Player 1 gets the higher number, he or she adds the two numbers on the dice and takes that score. If Player 2 rolls the higher number, he or she subtracts it to find the difference between the two numbers on the dice and takes that score. If both roll the same number, neither one scores any points. After rolling the dice 10 times, they total their scores to see who won.

■ Choose a student to be your partner and model playing the game. On the board write *Player 1* and *Player 2* to head two columns. Ask another child to keep score by recording the points for each round in the correct columns.

■ Have all of the students play *The Plus and Minus Game,* decide if it's a fair or unfair game, and write letters to the game company explaining whether they would recommend the game and why. To help the children, write on the board the format for a letter. Also, list the following questions to help guide the students' thinking:

Do you recommend this game?
Do you think children would like this game? Why or why not?

■ When the pairs have completed their letters, have them prepare to read them to the class, and then ask for volunteers to do so.

Part 2: The New Plus and Minus Game

■ Give the students the directions for *The New Plus and Minus Game.* Explain that this game is played the same way, except that when both players roll the same number, Player 2 adds the *sum* of these two numbers to his or her score.

■ Write on the board:

<u>Player 1</u>   <u>Player 2</u>

Tell the students to play one game, each rolling 10 times, and write statements about their findings. Then they record their total scores in the two columns on the board.

■ When all students have played the game, initiate a class discussion. Ask students whether this game is more fair than the version they played the day before. Have students explain the reasons for their opinions.

■ Discuss the results on the class chart.

FROM THE CLASSROOM

After the class had spent a few days working independently on menu activities for a good part of each math period, I introduced this whole class lesson to change the pace. The lesson would prepare the children for two additional menu tasks.

I began by talking about how some people invent games. "When they think they have a good idea," I said, "they send the directions for their game to a game company. Producing a new game requires a large investment of money, and the company needs to be sure that the game is good enough to manufacture and sell. To decide, they have their research department test new games. They ask the researchers to play the game and see if the directions make sense. They might even test the game with some children. The job of the researchers is to make a recommendation: Should the company produce this game or not?" My explanation was long, but the students were interested.

I explained, "Today, you'll become research teams and test a new game. After trying the game, you will write letters to the president of the game company telling what you think about it."

"What's the game?" Wade called out.

"It's called *The Plus and Minus Game,*" I said. "It's a game for two players. The only materials you need are a pair of dice and a sheet of paper for keeping score."

I then explained how to play. "First, decide who is Player 1 and who is Player 2. Then you each roll one die. If Player 1 rolls the higher number, he or she *adds* the two numbers and takes that score. If Player 2 rolls the higher number, he or she *subtracts* to find the difference between the two numbers and takes that score. If you both roll the same number, neither one gets any points for that round. Roll the dice 10 times. Then find the total for each player and see who gets the higher score."

I asked Dylan to be my partner and Cecilia to keep score as we rolled the dice. Dylan was Player 1 and I was Player 2. Cecilia recorded the results of our 10 rolls and, with the help of the class, also recorded the totals.

Player 1	Player 2
9	1
7	3
9	4
6	2
4	
10	
Total 45	10

The children seemed to understand the directions, so I explained that they would play this game in pairs and then write their letters together. I was about to tell them to begin playing when several students had something to say.

I called on Chris.

"I already know this game stinks." Several others agreed.

"Why don't you think this is a good game?" I asked Chris.

He said, "It's obvious. Player 1 will always win if Player 1 gets to add and Player 2 does minus."

"Player 2 will never win," Kirk added.

"If I could always be Player 1, I'd like this game," Luisa chimed in.

Jack raised his hand and said, "I'd like to buy that game, so my auntie can be Player 2 and I'd be Player 1 so I can win her."

Holly said, "Why don't you change the game so that both players get to add?"

Dylan quickly added, "Or they both could take away."

I told the students that when they wrote their letters, they could include recommendations on how to change the game. "Your main job is to let the company know if you think this game is fair and if children will like it. Be sure to explain your ideas," I reminded them.

Even though the class seemed sure that Player 1 would always win, I felt they needed to play the game themselves. "Play the game with your partner. Then you'll know more about it and can judge whether you think it's fair," I said. I added *fair* and *unfair* to the Probability Words chart.

I also discussed with the class the use of the word *stinks* and whether this was appropriate to write in a letter to the head of the company. We generated a list of polite synonyms including: *not great, no way, don't like, unfair, a bad game, not good,* and *terrible.*

"After you play, you need to write your opinions in a letter," I said. I wrote on the board the format they were to use and suggested a way they might begin their letters.

Date

Dear _____ ,

We tried your Plus and Minus Game. _____

_____

_____

Sincerely,

_____ and _____

The Children's Writing

The writing in this lesson seemed easier for the students than most writing assignments. They knew how they felt about the game and during the discussion had heard explanations from several other students.

I noticed once again that working with a partner was difficult for a few students, and I talked with them, telling them, for example, when I noticed one person doing all of the work. This seemed to help.

When all pairs had completed their letters, I instructed them to prepare to read them aloud. "Decide how you will share the job," I said. "Who will read and who will hold the paper? Also, practice reading so you'll be ready when you come up to the front." I find that when I give students time and direction to prepare, the presentations go much more quickly and smoothly.

The students enjoyed standing up in front of the class to share their work. They seemed shy and proud all at once.

Nathan got right to the point: *Dear Milton Bradley, I do not like your game because it is unfair. Player 1 has a better chance of winning than player 2. Player 2 has to take away a certain amount while player 1 will add more to his amount.*

NOTE Encouraging children to work cooperatively with groups and with partners takes continual reinforcement and guidance. Children need to know that it's important that they learn to work together. Asking students to list the qualities of a good partner helps them learn how to work with others.

Nathan addressed his letter to Milton Bradley and explained why he thought *The Plus and Minus Game* was unfair.

Dear Milton Bradley,

I do not like your game because it is unfair. Player 1 has a better chance of winning than player 2. Player 2 has to take away a certain amount while player 1 will add more to his amount.

Rachel and Dylan were certain about their opinion of this game. They wrote: *Dear Parker Brother's, We tried your Plus and Minus game. We do not recommend this game. Children wouldn't like this game because it's not fair at all. Player 1 is always winning player 2.*

Jack and Luisa saw another problem: *Dear Parkerbrother, We tried your Plus and minus game. We don't think kids will buy this game becuse Player 1 always win. Everybody will always be player1.*

Jack and Luisa explained that everyone would want to be Player 1 in this game.

Dear Parkerbrother,

We tried your Plus and minus game. We don't think kids will buy this game becuse Player 1 always win. Everybody will always be player1.

Holly and Chris politely urged that the game be changed. They wrote: *Dear Parker Brothers: We don't really think this Game is fair. It is not fair because the first player always wins because the first player gets to add and the second player needs to minus. So please change the game so both players get to add.*

Holly and Chris suggested that both players be able to add.

Dear Parker Brothers:

We don't really think this Game is fair.

It is not fair because the first player always wins because the first player gets to add and the second player needs to minus. So please change the game so both players get to add.

Davy and Luisa had another suggestion for changing the game.

> Dear Fisher-Price,
>   We tried your Plus and Minus game. We want to change some thing from it. Because when ever player 1 gets a big number he or she adds, when player 2 gets a big number he or she has to minus. So it is better if both of the players have plus or minus.

Part 2: The New Plus and Minus Game

I told the class that the game company had rejected *The Plus and Minus Game*, but the inventor sent it back with a change in the rules. She thought it was an improvement. This meant that the game company needed the research teams once again.

"This is called *The New Plus and Minus Game*," I began. "Player 1 still adds the two numbers on the dice when he or she gets the higher number, and Player 2 still subtracts the two numbers when he or she gets the higher number. This time, however, if they roll the same number, Player 2 adds the total to his or her score." There was a chorus of "ahs," and many heads nodded. The children felt that this would be a better game.

I told the class, "Play at least one game of 10 rolls. Then, with your partner, decide if you think this game is more fair than yesterday's version. Write a statement on your score sheet. Then record your scores on the board so we can discuss the results."

I wrote the following headings on the board:

<u>Player 1</u>   <u>Player 2</u>

The children got to work quickly and used their results to form their opinions about the game. Their reactions to the game seemed to depend on whether they personally won or on the difference between the scores of Player 1 and Player 2.

When Cecilia and Dean played, Player 1 got 28 points and Player 2 got 26 points. They wrote: *This game is more fair. This game would be fun for kids.*

When Nathan and Timothy played, Player 1 got 74 points and Player 2 got 23 points. They wrote: *We still think that this game is unfair.*

From Chris and Aquilina: *Aquilina got 31 and I got 98, it is better. It is a little fair.*

Rachel and Dylan did not look at the total score. They played the game twice (two games of 10 rolls each). Player 2 won the first game and Player 1 won the second game. They wrote: *This game is better then the other time because it's fairer then usually. The time that wasn't fair was worse then this time. On the first time we played I won on the second time my partner won.*

Rachel and Dylan played two games and decided that the new game was fair.

> New Plus and Minus Game
>
> | Player 1 | Player 2 |
> |---|---|
> | 5 | 5 |
> | 9 | 10 |
> | +5 | 5 |
> | 19 | 4 |
> | | 4 |
> | | +2 |
> | | 31 |
>
> | Player 1 | Player 2 |
> |---|---|
> | 7 | 2 3 2 2 |
> | 9 6 | 3 2 2 |
> | 5 11 | 3 1 2 |
> | 7 10 47 | 6 2 1 |
> | 6 8 | 3 4 +35 |

> This game is better then the other time because it's fairer then usually. The time that wasn't fair was worse then this time. On the first time we played I won on the second time my partner won.

From Yasmine and Mitch: *I recommend this game because player 2 gets to add doubles so both players can win.*

After one game in which Player 1 got 23 points and Player 2 got 47 points, Mario and Kirk wrote: *This game is worse then before because player 2 will always win. We are sure just because player 2 will get the doubles.*

Lea and Fredric played, and Lea won with a score of 22 to 24. They wrote: *This game is worse because player 2 is more likely to win.*

After all the students had had a chance to play the new game and write their opinions, I called the class to the rug area. When I asked what the children thought of this new game, almost all hands went up.

I said, "Let's hear all of your opinions. You can read the statements that you wrote, and we can see if we agree."

I called on each pair of students to read a statement. It quickly became clear that there were mixed reactions about whether the game was more fair or not. Some were convinced the game was fair, others thought the game was still unfair, and others thought that this game was more fair than the first game but still not truly fair.

I asked the class, "What makes it a good game?"

"Sometimes Player 1 wins and sometimes Player 2 wins," Cindy said.

"They both have almost the same amount," Mitch added.

"I still think it's unfair," Nathan grumbled.

"Would you rather play the first version or *The New Plus and Minus Game?*" I asked.

"I'd rather play it the new way because it's more fair," offered Yasmine.

"The new way because sometimes Player 2 can add," said Lea.

"I like the old way. I like being Player 1 and I can always win," added Jack.

Aquilina said, "Game two because I could be Player 1 or Player 2 because sometime Player 1 wins and sometimes Player 2 wins."

Juliette summed it up when she said, "If you're buying a game, why buy a game you don't like?"

Cecilia and Dean felt the game would be fun for children.

New plus and minus game	
play 1	play 2
5	4
3	4
2	3
5	8
6	1
5	6
28	26
This game would be fun for kids	This game is more even

The mixed reactions of the children reflected two approaches to thinking about this new version. Player 2 does have more opportunities to score than in the previous game and more opportunities than Player 1. However, Player 1 has higher numbers to score.

After all the students had read their opinions, we looked at the board where students had recorded their scores for *The New Plus and Minus Game.* I circled the winner for each game. Player 1 had won eight times and Player 2 had won seven times.

Player 1	Player 2
22	(24)
23	(47)
(63)	15
27	(45)
(43)	23
(46)	38
(64)	18
19	(31)
(47)	35
28	(31)
(74)	23
(69)	40
(28)	26
9	(47)
14	(76)

"Now what do you think?" I asked. "Is this game more fair than the one we played yesterday?"

"Pretty close game," Davy said.

"In my game, I got 74 and Player 1 won." Nathan reported on his personal experience.

"It looks like sometimes they both win," Megan offered.

"I still think it's unfair," Nathan persisted.

At this age, children often tend to ignore evidence of a larger sample and cling to their own ideas, which often come from their individual results. With time and more experiences, children begin to see the power of basing decisions on data from large samples.

I told the class that we would talk more later about games and what made a good game.

Even though she lost her game with Aaron, Lauren thought *The New Plus and Minus Game* was fair.

New Plus and Minus
Game

Player 1	Player 2
3	11
4	12
2	8
+ 5	11
14	12
	+ 11
	76

I have less
and Aaron have more
and I thing this game is fair
player one and playtwo have a
certain of win,

CONTENTS

ASSESSMENTS

Assessing children's understanding is an ongoing process of collecting information about their understanding and their ability to use and communicate their knowledge. The ideas of probability are new to first and second graders, and most of the activities in this unit provide experience on which children can build later knowledge.

In the classroom, teachers learn about what students know from listening to what they say during class discussions, observing and listening as they work on independent activities, having conversations with individual children, and reading their written work. From a collection of observations and interactions, teachers gain insights into children's thinking and reasoning processes and learn about children's mathematical interests and abilities.

Teachers can assess students' understanding of probability during informal classroom observations and interactions. The following questions can help guide these informal assessments:

> Can a child distinguish between events that are likely or unlikely, possible or impossible, probable or improbable, certain or uncertain?

> Can a child use the terminology of probability appropriately when describing his or her thinking about activities in the unit?

> Can a child interpret measures of chance in real-world contexts, such as understanding the implication of a weather report that indicates an 80 percent chance of rain or knowing that 50-50 means the chance of winning is the same for both teams?

> Can a child interpret and use statistical data to make conjectures about probability activities?

> Can a child formulate theories about the probabilities of situations, such as "This is more likely because . . ." or "They're equally likely because . . ."?

To supplement the insights teachers gain from informal observations and interactions, the unit offers six formal assessments. *Strategies for 7 + 6* asks children to describe strategies for finding the answer to an addition fact. In *Likely and Unlikely*, children write what they think *likely* and *unlikely* mean and provide examples. After children have made spinners, spun them, and collected data, the assessment *100 Spins* asks them to extend their thinking by writing what they think would happen if they spun their spinners 100 times.

Throughout the unit, students use dice and playing cards for various investigations. *When You Turn Over Two Cards* and *When You Roll Two Dice* have students draw on their experiences with these materials to write about their thinking. In *Agree or Disagree with Sara,* students test a hypothesis by collecting data from rolling two dice.

Remember that assignments given for the purpose of assessing are just like other activities that ask children to consider a situation or mathematical idea. Therefore, the students should not be aware that they are being tested. As with all assignments, the message to the children is that the teacher wants to know what each of them is thinking.

ASSESSMENT Strategies for 7 + 6

FROM THE CLASSROOM

This assessment does not relate directly to probability but to students' experiences with adding numbers in the context of games such as *Empty the Bowl, Is It 10?* and *Is It 12?* The assessment asks students to figure out the answer to 7 + 6 and write three different ways to do it. While children are engaged in this assessment, it's possible to observe who knows the facts and who needs to figure out sums. Also, the children's writing gives valuable information about how children approach adding and their flexibility in thinking about addition. This assessment is appropriate after students have completed the *Addition Facts and Strategies* lesson. (See page 40.)

After I talked with the class about the 121 basic addition facts, I asked the children to write about their strategies for solving 7 + 6.

"After you figure out the answer and describe how you figured it out," I said, "try to think of two other ways someone could find the answer to this problem and write about them."

To give the students another way to approach the assignment, I said, "You might want to pretend you're explaining it to someone who doesn't know the answer."

"Do we work with our partner?" asked Lea.

"No," I answered. "For this assignment, I'd like to know what each of you thinks."

Knowing that they would all finish at different times, I added, "When you're finished, you may continue working on the menu."

As the children wrote, I went from table to table, encouraging them to write more than one way to solve the problem. I restated the question to several children in a different way. I asked some children, "What if you were trying to tell a first grader how to find the answer to 7 + 6?" I asked others to tell me how they might add 7 and 6. (If children can say it, they can usually write it.)

About one-third of the class finished writing in 15 minutes or less. After 30 minutes, I had all but six papers, and I worked with those children until I felt that they had done all they could.

When I looked at the children's papers, I sorted them into three piles: 8 children had three ways to solve the problem, 12 had at least one way besides counting, and 7 solved it only by counting.

Some students were confident with the mathematics and wrote methods that did not involve counting. For example, Lea's first method involved adding to 10 first. Her other two methods used doubles. She wrote:

1. I took the 7 and took 3 from the 6 that makes 10 and than I have 3 lefd 10 + 3 = 13

2. 7 + 7 = 14 and I Took away 1 and it makes 13

3. 6 + 6 is 12 + 1 = 13.

Fredric's solutions were similar to Lea's, but he wrote much more to explain the "make a 10" method. He wrote: *If you know 7 + 3 you would know 7 + 6 because 3 + 7 = 10 right then 7 + 6 is 13 because if 7 + 3 + 3*

= 13 a 3 will take away 6 then the 6 will have 3 more then 7 + 3 = 10 now you add a 3 and it = to 13.

Lea and Fredric each used the "make a 10" method and two ways of adding doubles.

> 7+6=
> 1. If you know 7+3 you would know 7+6 because 3+7=10 right then 7+6 is 13 because if 7+3+3=13 a 3 will take away 6 then the 6 will have 3 more then 7+3=10 now you add a 3 and it = to 13.
> 2. If you know 6+6 you just add a 1.
> 3. If you know 7+7 you just take away 1.

> 7+6=13
> 1. I took the7 and took 3 from the 6 that makes 10 and than I have 3 left 10+3=13
> 2. 7+7=14 and I Took away1 and it makes 13
> 3. 6+6 is 12+1 = 13

Jack's first method used doubles, and his second method used counting. He showed resourcefulness for his third suggestion. He wrote:

1. *I know 6 + 6 = 12 and then I add one = 13.*
2. *You should count Your fingers.*
3. *You should ask Your teacher.*

Jack found three distinct ways to solve the problem.

> 7+6=
> 1. I know 6+6=12 and then I add one =13.
> 2. You should count Your fingers.
> 3. You should ask Your teacher.

Davy could only think of two ways to solve the problem, and both involved counting. He wrote:

1. I counted on.
2. I counted 7 and I counted 6 and then I had 13.

Throughout the unit, I planned to continue to have children discuss how they figured out answers to the basic addition facts. Even children who already know their facts benefit from using addition in a variety of contexts and explaining their methods.

Both of Davy's methods involved counting.

> 7+6=___
>
> 1. I counted on.
> 2 I counted 7 and I counted 6 and then I had 13.

Juliette explained one way to get the answer and then showed two ways to get 13 that had nothing to do with the original 6 + 7.

> 7+6=13
>
> 1. 6+6=12 then if you add 1 more it makes 13.
> 2. if you had 16 and you took away 3 it would make 13.
> 3. if I had 17 markers and I gave 4 to my firend it would make 13.

CONTENTS

MENU ACTIVITIES

The eight activities selected for this menu give children further opportunities to learn about probability. These activities are intended to be done independently by children working individually or in pairs. They are designed both to be accessible to children with limited experience and ability and to challenge students with greater interest and ability. The menu is an opportunity for children to become self-reliant, cooperate, follow through, be responsible, and learn from one another. These are important lessons and life skills. And once students become accustomed to working on menu activities, the teacher is free to interact with individual students and groups.

The menu has several benefits in the classroom. Children can choose from a collection of activities that offer a variety of ways to think about probability and can return to activities of special interest to them. They benefit from repeating activities several times. As they become more familiar with each investigation, they are better able to make inferences and develop strategies based on their experience and the data they collect. The menu format also gives students the time they need to explore activities fully, without the time restraints of a single class period and without the pressure that they all have to finish at the same time.

Four activities on the menu are direct extensions of whole class lessons. *Empty the Bowl with 20* is a repeat of the *Empty the Bowl* activity done with the whole class, but this time the children use 20 tiles instead of 12. *Is It 12?* is similar to the whole class lesson *Is It 10?* and provides children with the opportunity to compare results from both games. As a follow-up to the *Likely–Unlikely* whole class lesson, *Likely–Unlikely Book* has each student make a book of probability events that relate to his or her own life and interests. *More Spinners* repeats the whole class lesson *Spinner Experiment* with a different spinner that produces different results.

The other four activities introduce children to new investigations that are natural extensions of other experiences in the unit. In *Roll One Die* and *Roll Two Dice,* children investigate probability while rolling dice. The *1 to 10 Game,* invented by two second graders, involves both chance and strategy and sets the stage for further exploration of games. For *Invent a Game,* the children create games that they share with one another.

The Importance of Class Discussions

While the menu activities provide experiences with probability ideas, class discussions help students express their ideas, learn about other students' ideas, and develop and strengthen their understanding. These discussions also provide teachers with opportunities to receive feedback about the activities and assess what the students have learned.

A class discussion is most beneficial after students have had time to work on a menu activity and engage with the probability ideas. The vignettes in the "From the Classroom" section for each menu activity contain valuable suggestions for leading class discussions. The situations described in these vignettes will not, of course, be the same in other classrooms, but they are representative of what typically occurs, and the teacher's responses are useful models for working with students during menu time.

Classroom Suggestions

The "Notes about Classroom Organization" section on pages 5–7 includes information about organizing the classroom for menus. Following are additional suggestions.

Because the menu activities relate to previous instruction in whole class lessons, students are somewhat prepared for them. However, menu activities need to be introduced carefully so that the children understand what they are to do. When children are clear about what is expected of them, they're more able to function as independent learners. Specific teaching directions are provided in the "Getting Started" section of each menu activity.

Also, it's best to introduce just one or two menu activities at a time. "A Suggested Daily Schedule" on pages 8–11 offers one plan for introducing menu activities and structuring menu time for the unit.

Giving clear directions is not always sufficient for helping children learn to work independently on a menu activity. You might need to review directions several times on different days to be sure that the children understand and remember what to do. For example, blackline masters for menu activities that require students to work in pairs are marked with a *P* in the upper right-hand corner; those that can be done individually are marked with an *I*. Children might need to be reminded from time to time that the directions for menu activities are available to them on the written menu tasks.

Observing the Children

When I first observe children working on or discussing menu activities, I focus on gathering several kinds of information. First, I'm interested in seeing how partners work together. How do they share the work? Do they take turns easily? Do they discuss what they're doing?

Second, for activities that require children to add, such as *Empty the Bowl with 20, Is It 12?* and *Roll Two Dice,* I check on students' facility and confidence with the basic facts. Do they "just know" most of their facts or do they count to find the answers? Are they all confident in their ability to add, or does one partner rely on the other?

Also, I'm interested in how students interpret their own data and generalize about class data. When we have class discussions, I know that I don't hear from all children, so conversations during menu time help me find out what individuals are thinking.

Providing Ongoing Support

From time to time, it's helpful to hold discussions about working with partners. Encourage students to talk about how partners can help each other. Ask children to bring up problems they've encountered and describe how they resolved them or ask the class for suggestions. You may want to report what you've observed about children working independently and cooperatively. These discussions are invaluable in helping children become productive learners.

Although students are encouraged to make choices and pursue activities of interest to them during menu time, they also should be required to try all of the menu activities. Be aware, however, that children will respond differently to activities. Not all children get the same value out of the same experiences; children will engage fully with some activities and superficially with others. This is to be expected and respected. Also, each activity can be revisited several times, and the menu gives children the opportunity to return to those activities that especially interest them.

FROM THE CLASSROOM

On the day before I planned to have the children choose activities from the probability menu, I posted the list of menu activities. (See page 170.) The menu list looked like this:

170

Probability Menu

☐ Empty the Bowl with 20

☐ Is It 12?

☐ Likely–Unlikely Book

☐ Roll One Die

☐ More Spinners

☐ Roll Two Dice

☐ The 1 to 10 Game

☐ Invent a Game

From *Math By All Means: Probability, Grades 1–2* · ©1996 Math Solutions Publications

"Today you'll prepare your menu folders," I began. "You'll do this with your partner."

Chris raised his hand and asked, "Do I have to work with Holly?"

"Yes," I responded. "You'll work with the person sitting next to you." The children had just changed seats two days earlier, and some of them had not yet developed smooth working relationships. We usually change seats at the beginning of each month, using a random method of picking playing cards that tell each student what table to move to.

I continued with the instructions. "Prepare your folder the same way you did for the first two units," I said, "and write the title and both of your names on the front. Also, use lined paper to make a list of the menu activities."

I wrote on the board what they were to do.

1. Prepare menu folder.
2. Write menu list.

This was the students' third experience with the menu format this year. During the first menu, they learned to make a folder using two pieces of 12-by-18-inch construction paper. They folded one in half "hot dog" style and one in half "hamburger" style. Then they inserted the "hamburger" sheet into the "hot dog" sheet and taped the two sheets together so that each folder had four pockets.

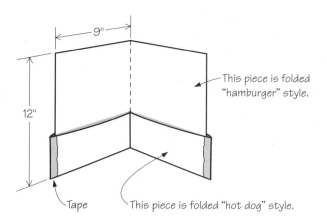

9"

12"

This piece is folded "hamburger" style.

Tape

This piece is folded "hot dog" style.

Also, the children had learned that the menu list is a way for them to keep track of the activities they do. On their menu lists, children put checks or tally marks alongside the names of menu activities each time they choose them.

Some children began by making their folders; others by making their menu lists. Some worked on the rug close to the posted menu list. Often one partner was reading and spelling while the other wrote. Because of their prior experience, the children had no trouble preparing their folders and menu lists, and it seemed to take no time at all.

The Next Day

To begin class, I gathered the children on the rug in front of the board. When they were settled, I pointed to the first task on the list. "A few days ago, you played *Empty the Bowl* with 12 tiles," I said. "Today you'll play it again using 20 tiles."

I pointed to the next task. "*Is It 12?* is similar to the game *Is It 10?*" I said. "Since you're already familiar with these two activities, we'll go over the directions quickly." I called the students' attention to the written directions I had posted. "What materials do you need for *Is It 12?*"

I called on Cecilia. "You need a partner," she said.

"How does Cecilia know that you need a partner?" I asked to give the others a chance to study the directions.

Several hands went up, and I called on Aaron.

"There's a *P* right here," he said as he jumped up to point to the corner of the game directions.

Even though the children have had experience with the menu format this year, I know that I must remind them regularly that the written directions can be helpful. If I forget, they lapse into being more dependent and relying on me to answer questions. My goal is to help them find other sources besides asking the teacher and learn to find answers on their own.

We continued reading the list of materials needed and the directions for *Is It 12?* I reminded the class that partners were to write both of their names and the title of the task on their paper.

"What do the directions say to do when you finish playing the game?" I asked.

"Count how many times the sums were less than 12, exactly 12, and greater than 12. Record the totals for each game on the class chart," Matt read.

I called the students' attention to the new chart on which they would record their data and to the completed chart for the whole class lesson *Is It 10?* I took time to have them review the results from *Is It 10?* and to predict what they thought would happen when they played *Is It 12?*

Next, we looked at the directions for *Empty the Bowl with 20.*

"The only thing different about this game is that you put 20 tiles in the bowl instead of 12," I told the students.

I modeled a game with Jack rolling the die and Megan taking out tiles while I recorded on the board. I wrote as Jack rolled:

$$5 + 2 + 4 + 1 + 5 + 6$$

Together we totaled the numbers, and I recorded the sum and the number of rolls it took to empty the bowl:

$$5 + 2 + 4 + 1 + 5 + 6 = 23 \qquad \overset{\text{Rolls}}{6}$$

"Play this game five times with your partner," I reminded the class. "After you finish five games, record tally marks on the class chart to show the number of rolls each game took."

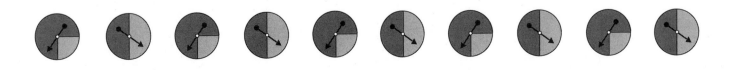

Then I colored in the boxes in front of the two tasks I had introduced and said, "These are the two activities you can choose from today."

Since each student would be working on menu activities with the same partner over the next few weeks, I thought that this would be a good time to have a discussion about what makes a good partner.

"Before you begin work, there's one more thing we need to discuss," I said. "First, I'd like you to return to your seats."

Once the students were seated and I had their attention, I asked, "Who can tell me something about what makes a good partner?" Many hands went up. I called on Cecilia.

"Someone who helps you," she said.

"They share," Mitch added.

"You take turns," Juliette said.

"A good partner doesn't fool around," Chris said.

"It sounds as if many of you know what makes a good partner and how to be a good partner," I told them. "Before you get started today, you and your partner should agree on the activity you'll do and who will do what. Once you've decided, you may get your materials and begin."

Over the Next Several Weeks

After students work on the menu for a couple of weeks, I make time to check their progress. I do this during menu time by pulling up a chair next to children and perusing their menu folders. Often a check means that they have started a task rather than completed it. Getting the children to follow through on their work and know when they have done each activity at least once takes a lot of nudging and reminding.

Throughout the unit, I make many decisions to keep children actively engaged in the investigations and in the various discussions. I have to decide how to balance whole class lessons with independent menu activities, when to stop the class so that the cleanup goes smoothly and isn't rushed, how many new activities to introduce at one time, when it's time to discuss each activity, how long to have the students talk about the results of their investigations, and when to have discussions about how to work with a partner.

There are days during menu time when I look around and say "This is just how it's suppose to be." Everyone is engaged, the class is calm, children are helping one another, and everyone knows what to do. But there are those other days when it seems too noisy to be productive, several children have trouble staying focused, and everyone seems to have forgotten how to do the activities. These are the times when I have to decide how to redirect the energy. Has the class been working independently too long? Do they need to review the directions for an activity? Is it time to pose a new question to investigate? Should we stop early and share our progress? It's important for all of us as teachers to learn to find the balance for ourselves and our students.

Even with the logistical challenges, I know that menu time is worth the effort. When menu time is going smoothly, I can interact with my students and learn about them in ways that are impossible when I'm trying to keep the attention of 28 children focused on one activity, with me at the head of the class.

MENU ACTIVITY

Overview

Empty the Bowl with 20

This activity is an extension of the whole class lesson *Empty the Bowl.* (See page 22.) In this activity, pairs of students play the game using 20 Color Tiles instead of 12. One partner rolls the die to determine how many tiles to remove from the bowl and then removes the tiles. The other partner records the numbers rolled and keeps track of the number of rolls it takes to empty the bowl. Once the bowl is empty, the students add the numbers, practicing their addition skills. They play five games, switching roles for each game, then record on a class chart the number of rolls it took to empty the bowl for each game. The class compares the data on the chart for *Empty the Bowl with 20* to the data on the chart from the whole class lesson.

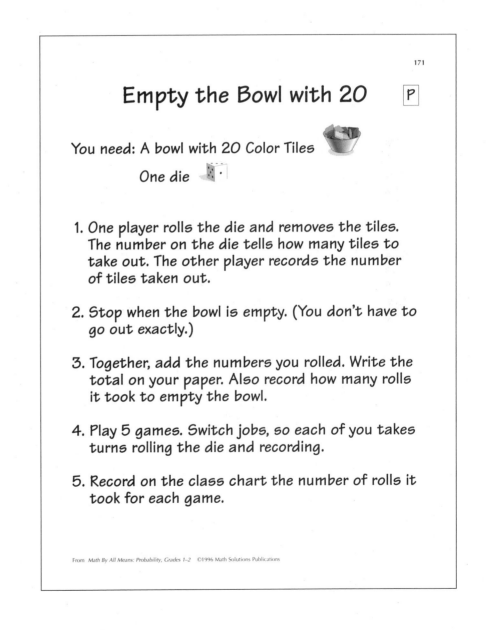

171

Empty the Bowl with 20 [P]

You need: A bowl with 20 Color Tiles

One die

1. One player rolls the die and removes the tiles. The number on the die tells how many tiles to take out. The other player records the number of tiles taken out.

2. Stop when the bowl is empty. (You don't have to go out exactly.)

3. Together, add the numbers you rolled. Write the total on your paper. Also record how many rolls it took to empty the bowl.

4. Play 5 games. Switch jobs, so each of you takes turns rolling the die and recording.

5. Record on the class chart the number of rolls it took for each game.

From *Math By All Means: Probability, Grades 1–2*   ©1996 Math Solutions Publications

Before the lesson

Gather these materials:
■ Small bowls (large enough to hold 20 Color Tiles), one per pair of students
■ Color Tiles, 20 per pair of students
■ Dice, one die per pair of students
■ One sheet of chart paper, titled "Rolls to Empty the Bowl with 20"
■ Blackline master of menu activity, page 171
■ Class chart from whole class lesson *Empty the Bowl*

Getting started

■ Discuss the rules for *Empty the Bowl with 20* with the class. Explain that the students are to play *Empty the Bowl*, except that in this game they start with 20 tiles in the bowl instead of 12. For each game, one partner records while the other rolls the die, and when the bowl is empty they find the total of their numbers.

■ Post a sheet of chart paper titled "Rolls to Empty the Bowl with 20." Explain to the students that after playing five games, they should record tally marks on the class chart to show the number of rolls each game took.

■ Ask the class: What is the fewest number of rolls possible to empty the bowl? Why? What is the greatest number of rolls? List the numbers from 4 to 20 down the left side of the chart.

```
┌─────────────────────────┐
│     Rolls to Empty      │
│    the Bowl with 20     │
│  4                      │
│  5                      │
│  6                      │
│  7                      │
│  8                      │
│  9                      │
│  10                     │
│  11                     │
│  12                     │
│  13                     │
│  14                     │
│  15                     │
│  16                     │
│  17                     │
│  18                     │
│  19                     │
│  20                     │
└─────────────────────────┘
```

■ A few days later, when all of the children have recorded on the class chart, ask them to examine the data and report what they notice.

■ Ask the students how they might finish the sentence: "When you play this game, you will most likely . . . " Give all who volunteer the chance to express their ideas.

■ Post the class chart from the whole class lesson *Empty the Bowl* and ask the class to compare that data with the data from *Empty the Bowl with 20.*

FROM THE CLASSROOM

"You've already learned how to play this game, so you're familiar with the directions," I said, calling the students' attention to the enlarged directions for *Empty the Bowl with 20.*

"Who knows what you need to play this game?" I asked.

"You need a partner," Dylan called out.

"What else?" I asked, and called on Cindy.

"Twenty tiles in a bowl," she responded.

"And dice," Fredric added.

"How many dice do you need?" I asked.

"Just one die," Lea said, with an emphasis on *die.*

"That's right," I said to stress that for this activity only one die is used. "The only thing that's different about this game is that you put 20 tiles in the bowl instead of 12," I added.

I modeled a game with Jack rolling the die and taking out tiles while I recorded on the board. I wrote as Jack rolled:

$$5 + 2 + 4 + 1 + 5 + 6 = 23$$

"Let's see," I said as I pointed to individual numbers, "the 5 and 5 are 10, and the 6 and 4 make another 10. How much is that?"

"That's 20," answered Timothy.

"I still have to add the other two numbers," I said pointing to the 2 and the 1. "What is the total?"

"Twenty-three," several students answered.

I recorded the total and the number of rolls it took to empty the bowl:

$$5 + 2 + 4 + 1 + 5 + 6 = 23 \qquad \begin{matrix} \text{Rolls} \\ 6 \end{matrix}$$

I posted the sheet of chart paper titled "Rolls to Empty the Bowl with 20."

"Play the game five times with your partner," I told the children. "Then come up and record tally marks on the chart to show how many rolls it took to empty the bowl each time you played. What numbers should I list on the chart?"

"You don't have to write a 1 or a 2," Nathan said.

"Why?" I asked.

"Because you can't empty the bowl in one or two rolls," he answered.

"You have to roll at least four times," Luisa said.

"What would you have to roll?" I asked.

"If you roll four 6s, that would be 24," she said.

"You could roll four 5s, too," Megan added.

I wrote on the board:

$$6 + 6 + 6 + 6 = 24$$
$$5 + 5 + 5 + 5 = 20$$

Then I asked, "Are there any other ways you could empty the bowl in four rolls?"

Several hands went up. I called on Juliette.

"You could also have 6 plus 6 plus 6 plus 2 equals 20," she said.

I added this possibility to the board.

"Two 5s and two 6s make 22," Matt said, and I wrote his contribution on the board.

"What's the most number of rolls it could take?" I asked.

"Twenty, if you're really unlucky," Mario said. "You'd have to roll all 1s."

I listed the numbers from 4 through 20 down the side of the chart and put a tally mark next to the number 6 for the sample game Jack and I had played.

"How many tally marks will you and your partner write on the chart?" I asked.

"Five," several students called out.

"Why?" I prompted.

"Because we have to play five games," answered Nathan.

"Do we have to play this game today?" Kirk asked.

"No," I said. "You'll have several days to put your results on the chart. Today you can play this game or *Is It 12?*"

Observing the Children

As I walked around the room I noticed that several pairs of children were playing *Empty the Bowl with 20*. Lea and Fredric had just finished their first game by rolling a 6 to empty the bowl. They had written on their paper: *5 + 2 + 6 + 5 + 6*.

"Oh, no!" Lea exclaimed. "That's more than 20. There were 2 tiles left before you rolled the 6, so that was 18. So, 19, 20, 21, 22, 23, 24." Lea wrote the total on their paper. Rather than adding the five numbers, Lea found the sum in a way that made sense to her. Knowing that 2 tiles left in the bowl meant that 18 had been removed was an indication of Lea's confidence.

Across the table from Lea and Fredric, Davy and Luisa had written *3 + 4 + 2 + 5 + 3 + 4*. I watched Luisa record *= 21* without hesitation.

"How did you know so quickly that the total was 21?" I asked her.

"There were only 3 more left in the bowl," Luisa responded, "so when Davy rolled a 4, I knew it equaled 21."

Often when I stop at a table to watch children playing a game, I get drawn into the discussion.

"Ms. Tank, don't 14 and 5 make 21?" Cindy asked. "No, 20?" she corrected herself.

"Well, I know that 15 plus 5 is 20," I said.

Cindy showed no response or sign of understanding how my statement could be of use to her in adding 14 and 5. I tried a different approach. I asked, "If you have 14, how many more do you need to make 20?"

Cindy and Rachel began counting on their fingers from 14 to 20.

"Six," they both said.

"So," I responded, "if you know that 14 and 6 are 20, what do you think 14 and 5 are?"

"Nineteen," Cindy said after a few seconds.

"Look, Ms. Tank," Juliette said when I stopped at her table. "It goes 3 plus 1 plus 3 plus 1 plus 3." Juliette was pleased with the pattern she'd noticed.

Juliette did all the recording for the six games she played with Noelle.

Empty the Bowl 20	Rolls
1. 1+5+2+6+4+3=21	6
2. 6+4+4+2+5=21	5
3. 3+6+1+5+1+4=20	6
4. 3+1+3+1+3+3+ +4=21	8
5. 3+2+1+5+5+4=20	6
6. 2+6+4+5+3=20	5

Kirk and Mario were having a problem recording the results from their five games on the class chart. They called me over.

"Kirk recorded all of our tallies," Mario complained. I remained quiet to see if Kirk had anything to say.

"I didn't think he wanted to write on the chart," Kirk said.

"Now that you know Mario wants to do his share, what can you do?" I asked them both.

Kirk looked at the chart and realized that he couldn't erase since they had used a marking pen.

Mario said, "We have to play another game."

Kirk did not look happy about this but knew that it was a fair solution. They returned to their table and began another round.

Luisa and Davy played 10 games and took turns recording, numbering each one.

Luisa

Empty the Bowl

1. 3+4+4+1+3+2+2+6+ ROLLS 8
4. 5+1+3+3+5+5 ROLLS 6
6. 2+6+3+6+3 ROLLS 5
7. 4+6+6+5+ ROLL S4
9. 4+5+6+6- Rolls 4

Davy

2. 1+4+4+5+4+2 Rolls 6
3. 6+5+6+3+6+1+5 RoLLS 8
5. 6+5+2+2+6
8. 2+1+3+3+4+2+ ROLLS 5
ROLLS 7
10. 6+6+5+4 RoLLS4

A Class Discussion

One afternoon about a week later, I told the class, "You all need to complete *Empty the Bowl with 20* and be sure to record your tally marks by the end of the day. We'll talk about our results tomorrow."

I then posed a problem. "If every pair of students draws five tally marks on this chart, how many tally marks should there be?" I asked. "What do you need to know to figure this out?"

"How many kids there are," Timothy said.

"You need to know how many pairs," Luisa added.

"We know there are 30 students," I said. "How many pairs are there?" Several students raised their hands.

"Before I call on someone, talk to the person next to you about how many pairs you think are in our class," I said.

After a few minutes, I repeated the question. This time more hands went up.

"There's 15 pairs," Megan said.

"How did you figure that out?" I asked.

"Half of 30 is 15," she said.

"So, if each pair of students draws five tally marks on the chart and there are 15 pairs in the class, how many tally marks will we have on the chart when all the results are posted?" I asked.

"You could count by 5s," Lea offered. "You have to do it 15 times."

"Use the calculator and just do 5 times 15," Mario said matter-of-factly.

"If you know 10 5s make 50, you just count 5 more 5s, and that makes 75," Chris added.

I asked for volunteers to figure out how many tally marks were on the chart and how many more we needed. I chose Davy, Luisa, Timothy, and Nathan.

"When you all agree on the answer, let me know and I'll have you report to the class," I told them.

I asked the rest of the class to continue working on the menu. "If you haven't completed *Empty the Bowl with 20*," I said, "do it first, so your results will be on the class chart for our discussion."

Davy, Luisa, Timothy, and Nathan reported to the class that there were 45 tally marks on the chart. Nathan added that we needed 30 more.

At the beginning of math time the next day, I asked the children to sit on the rug so we could look at the *Empty the Bowl* data. Several children scrambled to record their results for *Empty the Bowl with 20*. I posted both class charts—*Rolls to Empty the Bowl* from the whole class lesson and *Rolls to Empty the Bowl with 20* from the menu activity.

Once the students were settled, I focused them on the chart from the menu activity. "What do you notice about our results?" I asked.

"They go from 4 to 10," Chris offered.

"Six got the most," Natalya said.

"And 7 was next," Davy added.

"Let's write the totals for all the numbers that have tally marks," I suggested. The students helped me count, and I put the totals to the right of each set of tally marks.

Next, I asked, "How would you finish this sentence: When you play this game, you will most likely . . . ?" I called on Cecilia.

Rolls to Empty the Bowl with 20		
4	⁙	5
5	⁙ ⁙ ⁙ ⁙	20
6	⁙ ⁙ ⁙ ⁙ III	23
7	⁙ ⁙ ⁙ ⁙ I	21
8	⁙ ⁙	10
9	II	2
10	I	1
11		0
12		0
13		0
14		0
15		0
16		0
17		0
18		0
19		0
20		0

Rolls to Empty the Bowl		
2	I	1
3	⁙ ⁙ ⁙ ⁙ ⁙ ⁙ I	31
4	⁙ ⁙ ⁙ IIII	19
5	⁙ ⁙	10
6	IIII	4
7		0
8		0
9		0
10		0
11		0
12		0

"When you play this game, you will most likely empty the bowl in less than 10 rolls," she said.

"Another idea?" I asked.

"When you play this game, you will most likely need five, six, or seven rolls," Matt said.

"What if you played another game right now?" I probed. "Raise your hand if you think the bowl will most likely be empty in four rolls." No hands went up.

"How about five rolls?" I asked. There were 3 hands.

"How many think six rolls?" I continued. I counted 12 hands.

"What about seven rolls?" About 10 hands went up.

"Eight rolls?" I asked. This time 2 hands went up.

"Does anyone think it will take more than eight rolls?" I asked. Rachel raised her hand.

"If you want to be sure the bowl will be empty, you need to roll 20 times," she explained.

"But nobody rolled more then 10 times on our chart," Luisa said.

"Rolling 20 1s is almost impossible," Kirk added.

"It's very unlikely," Natalya said quietly.

I wanted the class to compare the data from the whole class lesson *Empty the Bowl* with the data for *Empty the Bowl with 20*.

"Here are the results from *Empty the Bowl* when we played with 12 tiles," I said, pointing to the chart from the whole class lesson. "I'm curious about how these two games compare," I said. "What do you notice about how the results are alike and how they are different?" The children studied the data from the two games.

"Tell the person next to you something you notice," I encouraged.

After giving the children time to talk to one another, I called on Lea.

"In both games, there's no tallies on the higher numbers," she offered.

"Both charts go like upstairs and downstairs," Davy said, motioning with his finger.

"Three won on the first chart and six won on the other," Natalya said.

"For *Empty the Bowl* with 12 tiles, 6 is the most rolls it took; for *Empty the Bowl with 20,* 10 rolls is the most," Nathan told us.

"Why do you think there are no tally marks on the higher numbers?" I asked.

"When you roll the die, you don't always roll 1s," Cecilia suggested.

"Sometimes you roll big numbers and take out more tiles," Kirk said.

As the children returned to their seats, I overheard some of them still talking about what was more and less likely to happen with the game. Children benefit from being asked to think about data, interpret it in the context of an activity they know, and share their ideas.

(left) Lea and Nathan's paper showed that they played five times but made two addition errors.

(right) Aquilina and Dylan played five times, then wrote a likely statement about the game.

Empty the Bowl	Rolls
1. $1+4+4+4+1+5+4=23$	7
2. $5+3+4+2+4=21$	6
3. $6+6+4+2+6=25$	5
4. $1+4+6+4+6=21$	5
5. $3+1+2+6+5+1+4=21$	7

Empty The Bowl	Rolls
$3+5+3+1+5+3=20$	6
$2+6+5+4+6=23$	5
$1+1+5+3+6+3+3=22$	7
$5+5+4+3+6=23$	5
$6+6+3+4+6=25$	5

It is likely to get 6,5 or 7 rolls to empty the bowl.

MENU ACTIVITY

Is It 12?

Overview

Because they played *Is It 10?* in a whole class lesson (see page 32), students are familiar with the directions and the format for recording the results for *Is It 12?* After reviewing what happened when they played *Is It 10?* they predict what might happen when they play *Is It 12?* In pairs, they play the game at least once. Later, they compare the results of both games. Playing this game gives children practice recognizing sums that are less than 12, exactly 12, and greater than 12. Observing students gives the teacher opportunities to assess their facility with basic addition facts.

The data collected during this activity are used in the assessment *When You Turn Over Two Cards.* (See page 89.) In a homework assignment (see page 164), students teach this game to someone at home, play the game at least once, and bring in the results for class discussion.

172

Is It 12? P

You need: A deck of playing cards ♠

1. Use only the ace, 2, 3, 4, 5, 6, 7, 8, 9, and 10 cards.

2. Shuffle the deck and deal all of the cards so both partners have the same amount. Each player keeps the cards in a pile, face down.

3. Each player turns over the top card. Together, add the two numbers aloud. Remember that ace = 1. Decide if the total is less than 12, exactly 12, or greater than 12.

4. Record the results like this:

Less than 12	Exactly 12	Greater than 12
4 + 5 = 9	7 + 5 = 12	10 + 4 = 14

5. Continue for all the cards.

6. Count how many times the sums were less than 12, exactly 12, and greater than 12. Record the totals for each game on the class chart.

From *Math By All Means: Probability, Grades 1–2* ©1996 Math Solutions Publications

Before the lesson

Gather these materials:
- ■ Decks of 40 playing cards (ace–10 of each suit), one deck per pair of students
- ■ One sheet of chart paper, titled "Is It 12?" and with three columns labeled "Less than 12," "Exactly 12," and "Greater than 12"
- ■ Blackline master of menu activity, page 172
- ■ Class chart from whole class lesson *Is It 10?*

Getting started

■ Explain to the students that they will play *Is It 12?* a game that is similar to *Is It 10?* With the class, read and discuss the directions.

■ Post the class chart titled "Is It 12?"

Is It 12?		
Less than 12	Exactly 12	Greater than 12

■ Remind the children to record the results for each game on the chart. (They'll use the data later for the assessment *When You Turn Over Two Cards.*)

FROM THE CLASSROOM

I enlarged and posted the blackline master for *Is It 12?* (see page 172) and asked the class to look at the directions.

"This menu activity is just like the game *Is It 10?*" I said. "Read the directions to yourselves to check the materials you'll need to play *Is It 12?*" After a few moments, several hands went up, and I called on Cecilia.

"You need a partner," she said.

"How does Cecilia know that you need a partner?" I asked to give the others a chance to study the directions.

Several hands went up, and I called on Aaron.

"There's a *P* right here," he said as he jumped up to point to the corner of the game directions. I then called on Aquilina.

"You need a partner and a deck of cards," she said with certainty.

"Then what?" I asked.

"Take out the face cards," Mario offered.

"Shuffle the cards and deal them," Dean said.

"Who would like to read what direction number 3 says?" I asked. I called on Jack.

"Each player turns over the top card. Together, add the two numbers aloud. Remember that ace equals 1. Decide if the total is less than 12, exactly 12, or greater than 12," he read aloud.

I nodded, then explained the rules further. "When you turn over the two cards, be sure to say the sum aloud. If you turn over a 6 and an 8, for example, say: '6 plus 8 equals 14.' Find a way to work together to figure out the sum of the two numbers. I don't think it would be a good idea for one person to say all of the answers. Why do I think that?" I asked.

"The other person won't get to learn anything," Rachel said.

"Yes," I said, "the game is an opportunity for all of you to practice adding."

I then explained to the children how they were to record. "You need to get your paper ready before you start playing," I said, pointing to the example on the enlarged menu directions:

Less than 12	Exactly 12	Greater than 12
$4 + 5 = 9$	$7 + 5 = 12$	$10 + 4 = 14$

"Remember to put both of your names and the title 'Is It 12?' on the paper," I added. I didn't feel it was necessary to model how to set up their papers and keep score because their experience with *Is It 10?* was still fresh in their minds.

"What do the directions say to do when you finish your game?" I asked.

"Count how many times the sums were less than 12, exactly 12, and greater than 12. Record the totals for each game on the class chart," Matt read. I taped the class chart to the wall nea ⊥ne front of the room.

Then I called the students' attention to the chart with the class data for *Is It 10?* and asked, "Who remembers what we found out when we looked at our data for *Is It 10?*"

"We usually got greater than 10 and usually didn't get exactly 10," Luisa told us.

"What do you think our results will be when we play *Is It 12?*" I asked. "Before I call on you for your prediction, share your thinking with the person next to you." I had the students discuss among themselves to engage more of them in thinking. After they'd had time to talk with one another, I called on Juliette.

"It's just probability," Juliette said matter-of-factly. "You can't tell what's going to happen."

"We think less than 12 will win because 12 is a bigger number than 10," Chris said.

"I think less than 12 too because it's harder to get more than 12," added Lea.

"We won't get many exactly 12s," said Jack.

"When we played *Is It 10?* many people got less than 10 six times," I said. (See chart on page 38.) "How many times do you think we'll usually get less than 12?"

"Around eight," Nathan offered quickly.

"I think about 19," Dean said.

"Where the less-than-10 column says 7, I think we'll get 9. Where there's an 8, I think 10," Cecilia said, being very specific.

"So you think there will be about two more in the less-than-12 column?" I asked, restating Cecilia's theory. Cecilia nodded.

"After you have a chance to play *Is It 12?* we'll look at the two charts and see how they compare," I said.

Observing the Children

Is It 12? was a popular choice during menu time. One day I pulled my chair up to the table where Ivy and Wade were just beginning to turn over cards. They had neatly prepared their paper and each had half of the cards. They turned over a 7 and an 8.

Wade said, "More than 12."

Ivy wrote *7 + 8* in the "Greater than 12" column and passed the paper to Wade. He wrote *= 15* to show the sum.

Next they turned over a 9 and a 7. Wade pointed to the "Greater than 12" column. Ivy wrote *9 + 7* and passed the paper to Wade to record the total.

I began to wonder if they had agreed to this arrangement for sharing the work because Ivy didn't know the facts. I decided to watch a little longer before saying anything.

Next, they turned over a 10 and a 2.

"That's 12!" Wade said, excited that they had turned up two cards that added exactly to 12.

Ivy wrote *10 + 2* in the "Exactly 12" column and again passed the paper to Wade to write the sum.

"I notice that Wade is writing all of the answers and you're writing the two numbers," I said to Ivy. "Did you agree to work this way?"

"Yes," she said.

"I think it's a good idea for both of you to have a chance to write the answer or at least say it," I said.

They looked at each other as if they hadn't thought of this before. "What could you do to give Ivy a chance to give the answer?" I asked.

When they looked a little puzzled, I said, "Why don't you talk this over, and I'll come back to hear your ideas."

When I returned to their table a short time later, Ivy and Wade were ready with an idea.

"We decided to play two games and let Ivy say and write the answers next time," Wade said.

I liked their suggestion for two reasons. They would get more practice if they played the game a second time, and the second game would help Ivy become more familiar with some of the facts.

Timothy and Nathan turned over exactly 12 the same number of times as greater than 12.

Is It Twelve?

Less than 12	Exactly 12	Greater than 12
$10+1=11$	$6+6=12$	$10+5=15$
$7+2=9$	$8+4=12$	$9+9=18$
$5+2=7$	$2+10=12$	$7+9=16$
$4+4=8$	$9+3=12$	$5+8=13$
$7+1=8$	$5+7=12$	$10+6=16$
$1+7=8$		
$4+6=10$		
$8+3=11$		
$3+2=5$		
$3+1=4$		
⑩	⑤	⑤

Dylan and Matt are both quiet during class discussions, so I don't always know what they are thinking. I watched them as they played *Is It 12?* For each play, they silently turned over cards and recorded the answers.

"It's good to say the numbers out loud," I suggested. "What did you just write?"

Matt read, "7 plus 7 equals 14."

"You say the next one, Dylan," I said.

They turned over a 7 and an 8.

"Seven plus eight," Dylan said softly.

"Where will you write that?" I asked.

He thought for a while and said tentatively, "Greater."

"What is 7 plus 8?" I asked him. Dylan sat quietly.

"Write *7 + 8* in the 'greater than' column," I told him. I thought that writing it under the 7 + 7 that was already there might trigger a connection. Dylan wrote the addends but still sat quietly.

"How could you find the answer?" I asked.

"I could count," he said.

"Show me what you would do," I said.

"I'd go 7 and count 8 more—7, . . . 8, 9, 10, 11, 12, 13, 14, 15," Dylan counted, putting out eight fingers as he did so. He wrote the answer on their paper.

"Counting is one way to find an answer you don't know," I said, making sure he knew that this was allowable.

"Do you know what 7 plus 7 is?" I then asked.

"It's 14," he said.

"Well, 7 plus 7 is close to 7 plus 8," I said. "They're just 1 apart. That's how I know 7 plus 8 is 15." I hoped that sometime Dylan would make this connection.

Lea and Fredric were just completing a game when I moved to their table. "We only got 12 once," Lea said, pointing to the *10 + 2* they had written in the "Exactly 12" column.

"We usually got less than 12," Fredric added.

"I wonder how many other ways there are to get 12 using these cards," I mused. I knew that both Lea and Fredric had facility with numbers, and I wanted to encourage them to extend their thinking. They turned over their deck and began to fish through the cards looking for pairs that would add to 12.

"When you think you've found all the ways to make 12," I said, "write them down." I was curious to see if they could find all the ways and if they would record in an organized way.

Rather than have a class discussion at this time about the data, I linked a discussion of the data for *Is It 12?* and *Is It 10?* to the assessment.

Lea and Fredric turned over 12 only once and turned over less than 12 more times than greater than 12.

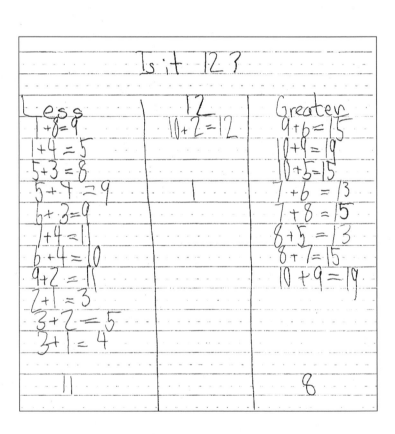

ASSESSMENT When You Turn Over Two Cards

FROM THE CLASSROOM

This assessment helps teachers learn more about children's ability to interpret and compare data. This assessment is appropriate after students have had a chance to play *Is It 10?* (see page 32) and *Is It 12?* (see page 83). Before assigning this assessment, have the children discuss the data from the *Is It 12?* class chart and compare that data with the class data from *Is It 10?* Then ask the children to use the data from both charts to answer the question: When you turn over two cards, what is likely to happen?

To introduce the assessment, I initiated a discussion about the data on the *Is It 12?* class chart.

Is It 12?		
Less than 12	Exactly 12	Greater than 12
10	0	10
10	3	7
10	1	9
10	3	7
9	3	8
10	3	6
10	2	8
10	3	7
10	4	6
12	0	8
9	1	10
11	1	8
8	4	8
13	2	5
11	1	8
10	5	5
12	0	8
12	3	5
9	2	9
9	5	5
11	1	8

"Let's look at what happened when we played *Is It 12?*" I said. "What do you think?"

"Lots of people said less than 12 would have more, and it did," Juliette recalled.

"Me and Nathan thought exactly 12 would win, but it didn't," Timothy reported.

"The numbers in the less-than-12 column are bigger than the numbers in the greater-than-12 column," Yasmine said in a quiet voice.

"Yeah, there are littler numbers on the more-than-12 side. Like 5s, 6s, and 7," Luisa noticed.

I posted the class chart from the *Is It 10?* game and asked the class to compare the results from *Is It 12?* and *Is It 10?*

Is It 10?		
Less than 10	Exactly 10	Greater than 10
6	1	13
6	0	14
6	1	13
7	1	12
8	1	11
4	3	13
7	2	11
8	3	9
6	1	13
6	3	11
7	1	12
6	2	12
5	4	11
6	4	10
4	5	11

"It's the opposite," Cecilia said.

"What do you mean by opposite?" I asked her.

"The less-than has bigger numbers on the *Is It 12?* chart and the greater-than has bigger numbers on the *Is It 10?* chart."

"Who could show us an example of what Cecilia means?" I asked, to clarify Cecilia's idea for some of the children.

Chris went up to the charts. "These are little and these are big," he said, pointing to the numbers in the less-than and greater-than columns on the *Is It 12?* chart. "And these are little and these are big," he said pointing to the numbers in the less-than and greater-than columns of the *Is It 10?* chart. "It's opposite," he added.

"We got exactly the opposite when we played both games," Mitch said, coming to the front and pointing to a row on each chart. "For *Is It 10?* we got 6, 4, 10, and for *Is It 12?* we got 10, 4, 6."

Is It 10?				Is It 12?		
Less than 10	Exactly 10	Greater than 10		Less than 12	Exactly 12	Greater than 12
6	4	10		10	4	6

I was amazed that he had remembered exactly which numbers he had written with his partner when the class played *Is It 10?* so long ago.

"I wonder what would happen if we play *Is It 11?*" I said.

"I think exactly 11 would win the most," Cecilia predicted. Several others nodded in agreement. (I didn't formally make this game an option, but some children chose to investigate it over the next several days.)

The charts showed a large amount of statistical data, and I wasn't sure that all of the children were following the discussion. I felt that the language used might be confusing to some students, particularly those for whom English was a second language. To find out how individual students would use the data to interpret the results of these two games, I asked them to write.

NOTE Hearing other ideas and approaches helps children expand their own thinking. When children write about their ideas they are able to clarify and cement their understanding.

I said to the students, "I'm interested in knowing what each of you thinks about what happens when you play *Is It 10?* and *Is It 12?*"

I wrote on the board:

<u>Is It 10? or Is It 12?</u>

When you turn over two cards, what is likely to happen?

I purposely made the question open ended and somewhat vague. I didn't want to lead the students to write what they thought I wanted them to say. Instead, I wanted to find out what the children had learned about the two games, based on their own experiences and their own interpretations of the class data. Also, there are always a few children who say little in class discussions, and one way of learning what they are thinking is to ask them to write.

The only other direction I gave was, "Just tell what you think."

The Children's Writing

The discussion was fresh in the children's minds, and each had played the game several times. They had no trouble writing what they thought. More than 20 of the children were able to communicate some understanding of the results of the two card games.

Wade focused on the likelihood of getting exactly 10 or exactly 12. He wrote: *It is likely that when you turn over two cards you will get some different number. Sometime you will get ten or twelve. It is unlikely that when you turn over 2 cards you just get ten. It is unlikely that you will get ten or twelve evrytime.*

Wade felt it would be unlikely to turn over exactly 10 or 12.

It is ten? or twelve

When you turn over 2 cards what happens?
It is likely that when you turn over two cards you will get some different number.
Some time you will get ten or twelve
It is unlikely that when you turn over 2 cards you just get ten.
It is unlikely that you will get ten or twelve evrytime.

Megan correctly interpreted the data from the two games. She wrote:
*When you turn over 2 cards you add them together they forms a number.
I [It] could be any number up to 20. It is likely that more than 10 will win
or less than 12.*

Megan summarized the game and correctly analyzed what was likely to happen.

> Is it ten? or twelve?
> When you turn over 2
> cards what happens?
>
> When you turn over 2 cards
> you add them together they
> forms a number. I could be
> any number up to 20.
> It is likely that more than 10
> will win or Less than 12.

Rachel was beginning to get a sense of the randomness of turning over
two cards but was tentative about her opinions and predictions. She wrote:
*Its a coincidence that somethig adds to 12 or 10 so I can't relly tell you
that there will be more of one, less of one or none of one. But I can tell
you what I think. I think that less than 12 will win. But don't know what
will happen with Is it ten—if we play it again.*

Rachel had a theory about playing *Is It 12?* but wasn't so sure about *Is It 10?*

> Is it 10? or 12?
>
> When you turn over a card
> What happens?
>
> Its a coincidence that somethig
> adds to 12 or 10 so I cant relly
> tell you that there will be more of
> one less ofone or none of one.
> But I can tell you what I think.
> I think that less than 12 will win.
> But dont know what will happen with
> Is it ten—if we play it again

Yasmine used a large sample of data—the class chart—to prove her theory based on her small sample. She wrote: *The frist card I turued over was Less then twelve. My second card was Less then twelve to. And my third card was More then twelve. I am more likely to have lass then twelve and the class chart prooved it.*

Yasmine based her theory on her own experiment but used the class data to "prove" it.

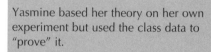

Is It 10 ? or 12 ?

When you turn over 2 cards What happens?

The frist card I turued over was Less then twelve.

My second card was Less then twelve to.

And my third card was More then twelve.

I am more Likely to have lass then twelve and the class chant prooved it.

Luisa tried to explain why when you turn over two cards you can get any number.

Is It 10? or 12?

When you turn over 2 cards what happens?

It can be any number. It can't always be ten or twelve. Its probability so it can be a ten, a five, it could be any number. You can't pick what it can be, but you can guess.

MENU ACTIVITY

Likely–Unlikely Book

Overview

This activity extends the *Likely–Unlikely* whole class lesson (see page 14) and integrates a language experience with math instruction. Students continue to think about events that are likely and unlikely and make their own books of statements that describe likely and unlikely events in their lives. When they finish their books, they share them with one another and take them home to read with their families.

174

Likely-Unlikely Book $\boxed{\text{I}}$

You need: 1 sheet of lined newsprint
         1 sheet of white construction paper
         Scissors

1. Use the lined paper to make a draft of your Likely–Unlikely Book. Fold the paper into 8 sections.

2. Write 4 likely statements and 4 unlikely statements, one in each box. When you finish your draft, place it in the "to be edited" box.

3. After your draft has been edited, make a book using a sheet of white construction paper. Title your book "Likely–Unlikely."

4. On each left-hand page, write one of your <u>likely</u> statements. On each right-hand page, write one of your <u>unlikely</u> statements. Draw pictures to illustrate your book.

From *Math By All Means: Probability, Grades 1–2*   ©1996 Math Solutions Publications

Before the lesson

Gather these materials:
- ■ 9-by-12-inch lined newsprint, at least one per student
- ■ 12-by-18-inch white drawing paper, one per student
- ■ Scissors
- ■ Blackline master of How to Make a Book, copies for students and one copy enlarged and posted (See Backline Masters section, page 173)
- ■ Blackline master of menu activity, page 174)

Getting started

■ Review the idea that some events in our lives are likely and some are unlikely. Refer to the statements from the *Likely–Unlikely* whole class lesson.

■ Introduce the *Likely–Unlikely Book* activity by telling the students that each of them will make a book about likely and unlikely events.

■ Demonstrate for the class how to fold the lined newsprint into eight sections to use for a rough draft of the *Likely–Unlikely Book.*

■ Talk about the purpose of a rough draft and tell the children to write four likely statements and four unlikely statements, one in each box.

■ Designate a "to-be-edited" box where students can put their rough drafts for your editing.

■ Show how to make a book from a sheet of 12-by-18-inch white paper.

1. Fold the paper in half twice as shown.

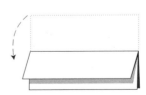

2. Fold the resulting rectangle in half in the other direction.

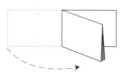

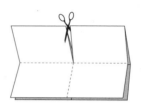

3. Partially open the paper and cut a slit as shown.

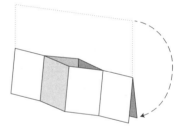

4. Open the paper and fold it in half lengthwise.

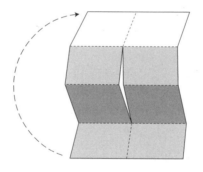

3. Gently push the side sections inward. The center should separate at the slit.

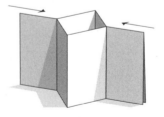

4. Keep pushing until the sections come together.

■ Model for students how to write the title and their names on the cover of the book. Using statements from the *Likely–Unlikely* whole class lesson, begin a sample book by writing a likely statement on the first left-hand page and an unlikely statement on the facing right-hand page. Tell the students that they are to illustrate each statement.

■ After each child has completed a draft, edit the draft with him or her. Each child then picks three likely statements and three unlikely statements to write and illustrate in his or her book.

■ Have the children place their finished books in a box so they are available for others to read. Near the end of the unit, have the children take their books home to share with their families.

FROM THE CLASSROOM

I posted the directions for this activity and explained to the students that each of them would make a book about likely and unlikely events. There was a murmur of excitement as there often is when the children are going to make a book.

"Let's read the directions, so you'll know exactly what to do," I said.

Juliette raised her hand. "We get to make our own books," she said.

"How does Juliette know that you will each make your own book?" I asked.

"There's an *I* in the corner," Mitch stated. "It means individual."

"We need two sheets of paper," Megan told us.

"Use the lined paper to make a draft of your *Likely–Unlikely Book,*" Kirk read.

"What does 'make a draft' mean?" I asked.

"It means make a practice book," Nathan answered.

"Yes, it's like a practice book," I said. "On lined paper, you'll write down your ideas for your *Likely–Unlikely* book. Then you'll read your ideas to me before you make the actual book."

"Fold the practice paper so that there are eight places to write," I told the class. I demonstrated how to fold a sheet of 9-by-12-inch lined paper for the rough draft.

"Then you should write four likely statements and four unlikely statements, one in each box. When you finish your draft, place it in this to-be-edited box," I explained as I held up a box. "I'll read your statements with you before you make your book." The children were accustomed to submitting rough drafts of their writing to be edited.

"Who remembers some of the events we mentioned last week that were likely or unlikely to happen?" I asked, wanting to refresh their memories. Several hands shot up. I called on Matt.

"We said the Giants would win every game," he said.

"Can someone restate Matt's idea and start the sentence with 'It is likely' or 'It is unlikely'?" I asked.

"It is unlikely the Giants will win every game," Natalya said.

"Does someone have an idea for a likely statement?" I asked.

More hands shot up, and I called on Cindy.

"It is likely we will make a book today," Cindy said, looking smug.

"Remember, each statement must include the word *likely* or *unlikely*," I said. "When you've all completed your books, you'll have a chance to read other students' books and also take yours home to read to someone."

I posted the enlarged, illustrated directions and demonstrated how to make a book. After I had made the book, Nathan's hand shot up.

"Can we make the book we learned how to make in Mrs. Genolio's class?" he asked.

I decided to let Nathan show the class how to make the kind of book he was talking about. I want students to know that they, too, are valuable resources—that the teacher isn't the only one with knowledge and experience.

As Nathan folded, cut, and refolded the paper to make the book he had learned to make in first grade, several other children also remembered how to do it. When he finished his demonstration, I told the students that they could choose the style book they wanted to make. I asked the children to raise their hands if they knew how to make a book Nathan's way. About five hands went up.

"If you want to make a book like Nathan's and you need help, ask one of the children who learned last year," I told them.

I showed the students how to put the title and their name on the cover of the book. I opened to the first two pages and wrote a likely statement on the left-hand side and an unlikely statement on the right-hand side. I used statements I had prepared for the *Likely–Unlikely* whole class lesson.

"After you write your statements, illustrate each one," I said.

"Can we put a picture on the cover, too?" Mario asked. I knew that Mario liked to draw. I responded that they could illustrate the cover if they wished.

Observing the Children

The children worked on their *Likely–Unlikely* books over the next few days. I noticed that Lea and Nathan willingly helped others make the book they had learned to make in first grade.

By the end of the second day of working on this menu, some students had put drafts for *Likely–Unlikely* books in the to-be-edited box. Over the next several days, I helped children edit their work. For example, I asked

Carla to read her statements to me. *"It is unlike that I am a cat,"* she read and then noticed that she had left off the *ly* on *unlikely*. I find that when children read their work aloud, they sometimes find mistakes they made or think about ways to improve their writing.

Several children had trouble with the structure of the unlikely sentences, sometimes putting in a double negative. For example, for another of her sentences, Carla wrote: *It is unlikely that my family are not moving.*

"Do you mean your family will probably not move?" I asked.

"Yes," she said, "we won't move."

"A better way to say that is: 'It is unlikely that my family will move,'" I told her. "Unlikely means you probably won't move." Carla changed the *are not* to *will be moving.*

After getting help with the spelling of the word *vacation,* Carla was ready to choose three likely statements and three unlikely statements and put them in the final book form. I checked off Carla's name on the class list I was using to keep track of whose books I had edited.

On her rough draft, Carla made several mistakes, which she corrected before writing her final book.

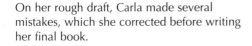

It is likely	It is unlikely
1. It is likely that I am not going to summer school.	It is unlikely that I am going to visit my cousin Rosanna.
2. It is likely that Francesca is my friend.	2. It is unlike that I am a cat.
3. It is likely that my mom and dad are going on vakacin.	3. It is unlikely that my family are not moving.

Lea began by reading her unlikely statements to me. She read: *"It is unlikely that I will ever like Mario."*

"It's not a good idea to put other children's names into your book," I said. "Everyone will have a chance to read your book, and I worry that this might hurt Mario's feelings."

"I don't know what to write," Lea responded.

"Is there a food you don't like very much?" I asked.

"Spinach," she said, and changed *Mario* to *spinach* on her paper.

When Chris read his draft to me, he found missing words. He also had a few spelling mistakes—*homerruns, allways,* and *resses.* After correcting these errors and writing a capital letter at the beginning of a sentence, Chris was ready to make his book. I checked off his name on my list.

Chris's rough draft had some spelling errors that he later corrected.

> It is likely
> It is likely that
> I will die before
> I am 100.
> it is likely that
> I will have broun
> eyes
> It is likly that
> we will go to
> resses,
>
> It is unlikely
> It is unlikely that
> I will allways
> hit homerruns.
> It is unlikely
> will be fat.
> it is unlikely
> will read sheep
> in a Jeep

I was able to edit about five papers a day with students during menu time, and, after a few weeks, I had checked off most of the names on the list and knew which students still needed to finish their drafts. I began checking on their progress. Two children had finished their drafts but had neglected to put them in the edit box; two couldn't find their papers anywhere; one was almost finished. I instructed these last three children to complete their drafts by the end of math time that day. To encourage them to focus on this work, I had them sit together at the back table.

The Children's Work

The finished books showed great variety. Some likely and unlikely statements revealed hopes and fears. Others reflected the predictability of everyday life. For example, Luisa wrote: *It is likely that I eat lunch at school. It is unlikely that It will snow in San Francisco.*

Megan wrote: *It is likely that I have some toys. It is unlikely that I have no friends.*

From Kirk: *It is likely that Michael Jordan is an excellent player in basketball. It is unlikely that school opens at 12:00 midnight.*

Other students' work showed a sense of humor. Nathan wrote: *It is likely that I will do my work. It is unlikely that I will sleep through class.*

Some children had likely and unlikely statements that were related. For example, Dylan wrote: *It is likely that I will go outside on a sunny day. It is unlikely that I will go outside on a rainy day.*

This example from Megan's book showed her confidence in real-life events.

Kirk coupled his love of sports with a humorous observation about school hours.

Dylan wrote related likely and unlikely events.

Lauren's unlikely statement revealed her idea of what makes a difficult math problem.

NOTE Often children can't complete math activities during math time. It's important to be flexible with the schedule and provide additional time for students to finish a discussion, an investigation, or their writing. Giving children more time or a special time to complete tasks conveys the message that their work is important.

About two weeks later, I checked on the progress of the books and found that most children had not fully completed them. Some had written a statement on each page but had not drawn illustrations; some had completed the sentences and illustrations on the first few pages but not in the entire book. I decided to give the class some extra time in the afternoon to complete their books. Taking this special time to have them all work on their books proved beneficial. They were proud of their finished products.

I put all the students' books in a box. They read one another's books and later took their own books home to read to their families.

The covers of these books conveyed wordless messages of likely and unlikely.

MENU ACTIVITY

Roll One Die

Overview

In this activity, students roll one die and keep track of the numbers that come up. *Roll One Die* helps children learn that it's equally likely for each number to come up on one die. After each child collects data for at least 25 rolls, the students generate questions about their results and then combine their data to answer some of those questions.

180

Roll One Die

I

You need: One die

1. Make a chart.

Roll One Die					
1	2	3	4	5	6

2. Roll the die at least 25 times.

3. Make a tally mark to keep track of each number you roll.

4. Record the total number of rolls for each number at the bottom of each column.

From *Math By All Means: Probability, Grades 1–2*   ©1996 Math Solutions Publications

Before the lesson

Gather these materials:
■ Dice, one die per student
■ Blackline master of menu activity, page 180

Getting started

■ Ask students what numbers can come up when they roll one die.

■ Draw a chart on the board with six columns numbered from 1 to 6.

■ Roll a die a few times and demonstrate how to record on the chart a tally mark for each number that comes up on the die.

Roll One Die					
1	2	3	4	5	6
I		II		I	

■ Tell the children to make their own recording charts, roll and record at least 25 times, and then write at the bottom of each column the total number of times each number came up.

■ When all the students have completed rolling dice and recording the results, initiate a discussion about their findings. Begin by asking for questions about what can happen when students roll one die. These questions should be ones they could investigate by examining the data they collected. Choose one of their questions for the class to investigate.

■ Have students work in small groups to combine their individual data. Record the groups' data on the board, and have the children find the total number of rolls for each number.

■ Ask the children to share their ideas about what the data show about the question they were investigating.

■ Write the following prompts on the board:

When you roll one die, it is likely that _____.
When you roll one die, it is unlikely that _____.

Ask the students to discuss the statements in their groups, then have volunteers share their ideas.

■ Direct the children to the class totals for each number. Introduce the idea that each number on a die is equally likely to come up, even though the data most likely won't show the same totals for each.

FROM THE CLASSROOM

I posted the directions for *Roll One Die* and called the children to the rug. When all were settled, I asked for a volunteer to read the directions aloud. I called on Juliette.

Then I asked, "If you roll one die 25 times, what do you think will happen?"

"I'd say 6 will probably win," Timothy said.

"I think 3," Kim offered.

"What makes you think that 6 or 3 will win?" I asked. Both children shrugged.

Kirk had a different idea. "You can't tell," he said. "The dice decide."

"Any number could win," Lea stated with authority.

"We'll see what happens when everyone rolls a die and records what comes up," I said.

To model what the children were to do, I taped a piece of lined paper to the board and wrote my name and *Roll One Die* at the top. "After you write your name and the title of the activity on your paper," I said, "you need to prepare a chart so that you can make a tally mark for each number you roll."

I drew vertical lines down the page to make six columns and numbered them from 1 to 6.

"When you've made your chart," I explained, "you roll the die and record a tally mark for each number that comes up." I modeled this for the class by rolling the die several times and making a tally mark in the correct column for each roll.

Roll One Die					
1	2	3	4	5	6
I		II		I	

"Find a way to be sure that you roll the dice at least 25 times," I continued. "You can roll more than 25 times, if you like. It's good to have as much data as possible. Keep your results in your menu folder, and we'll collect group results later."

I then had the children choose menu activities. *"Roll One Die* is now a choice on the menu," I said, as I colored in the square on the menu list. I directed the students to return to their seats and begin work.

Observing the Children

The classroom became busy as children got their folders and collected their materials. Some children chose to complete activities they had started the day before, but many chose to begin this new task.

I am always amazed at the different ways children work. At one table, Kirk drew his one die recording chart quickly, making the lines for the columns fairly straight, but being more concerned with getting on with collecting data. Across from Kirk, Dylan was using a ruler and carefully drawing the lines for his chart. Throughout the class, I observed that some children prepared their papers quickly and began to roll the die, while others were slow to get organized.

The children had no problem collecting the data for *Roll One Die.* Most of the students seemed to enjoy making their charts and rolling the die. Many stopped to count periodically to see how many times they had rolled. Some stopped rolling after 25 times, and others continued rolling.

Megan's 25 rolls resulted in 11 1s and no 6s.

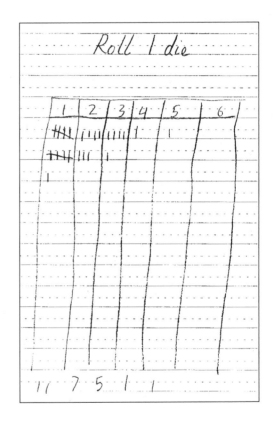

Carla and Lea worked side by side and cheered each roll. On each of their papers, 6 had the most tallies so far. I watched as they positioned their die with the 6 on the top and dropped it gently on the table calling out "6!" Sure enough, they both got a 6.

I interrupted and asked, "What are you trying to find out with this activity?"

"Which number will win," Lea answered.

"It looks as if you both want 6 to win," I commented. They smiled and nodded at each other.

"To collect the data scientifically, you need to try not to make a certain number come up," I said. "We're trying to find out if one number is more likely than any other, and the data must be collected fairly."

"Maybe we should start over," Carla said.

"That's a good idea," I agreed.

Timothy used checkmarks to record his rolls.

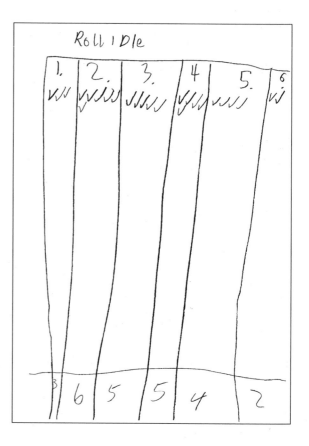

A Class Discussion

One day, after all the children had done *Roll One Die,* I asked them to take out their recording sheets. When they had their papers in front of them, I asked, "What questions could you ask about this experiment that we could investigate from the data you collected?"

"What number won?" Chris said.

I recorded Chris's question on the board and asked, "What else could you ask?"

"Will you and your partner get the same number every time?" Matt said. I wrote his question on the board underneath Chris's.

"Do you get low numbers sometimes and sometimes high numbers?" Natalya asked. I recorded her question.

Two more students offered questions, and I recorded them. The board now had the following list:

What number won?
Will you and your partner get the same number every time?
Do you get low numbers sometimes and high numbers sometimes?
Can you roll any number you want?
Is it possible to get the same number every time you roll the die?

"Let's find out about Natalya's question," I said and circled her question on the board. "With the data that you already have for *Roll One Die,* I think we can answer whether we sometimes get low numbers and sometimes high numbers."

I listed the numbers 1 through 6 on the board.

"Work in groups of four and combine your data," I said. "Count how many times you each rolled a 1, and find the total for your group. Do the same for 2, 3, 4, 5, and 6. Once you have the totals for your group, I'll call on each table to report how many times each number came up."

At table 6, Rachel took charge. On a new piece of paper she collected the results from each person at her table. She recorded this information by making tally marks as each person described his or her results. The group counted all of the tally marks.

Rachel took charge and collected the data from each person at her table.

At two other tables, students went to get calculators, and each person in the group worked individually to figure out different totals. At table 2, Natalya decided that each person would write his or her individual total on a new sheet of paper that Natalya had prepared. She patiently passed the paper to each member of her group.

I knew that some children would have trouble combining their information, but I wanted all of them to have experience sharing their results and working together to find the totals.

The children at some tables were very concerned about accuracy. They checked each person's paper carefully, added, and added again to be sure. At other tables, I had to push the children to check their totals.

When all the groups were satisfied with their totals, I asked for the children's attention. I called on each table to report orally as I recorded on the board. After all the tables had reported their data, the results looked like this:

	Roll One Die					
Table	1	2	3	4	5	6
1	15	16	15	15	19	15
2	12	18	10	20	21	18
3	14	22	22	16	8	18
4	20	17	15	22	17	19
5	20	16	14	10	25	15
6	15	20	14	19	17	16
7	19	19	22	10	15	17

The children were curious about the combined totals for all the groups. Many got out calculators and began to add the columns. There was confusion, however, because students came up with different totals for some of the same columns. Several children were determined to find the correct totals and stayed in the classroom through recess, working on each column until they were in agreement.

When the children returned from recess, I called their attention to the completed results and asked, "What were we trying to find out with all the data?" Natalya was the first to raise her hand.

"Who else knows the question we were trying to answer?" I asked, giving others a chance to recall.

I called on Carla. "Do you get low numbers sometimes and high numbers sometimes? It was Natalya's question," she said.

"Now that we have all of this information on the board, can we answer Natalya's question?" I asked.

"We need to add some more," Kirk said.

"What should we add?" I asked.

"The low numbers and the high numbers?" he responded tentatively.

"Which numbers are the low numbers?" I asked, wondering if we were all in agreement about that.

"Half are low and half are high," Aquilina said.

"I think 1, 2, and 3 are low numbers and 4, 5, and 6 are high numbers," Brian added. Many children nodded in agreement.

"Let's find the totals," I said.

Several children still had their calculators handy and found the totals for us:

Roll One Die						
Table	1	2	3	4	5	6
1	15	16	15	15	19	15
2	12	18	10	20	21	18
3	14	22	22	16	8	18
4	20	17	15	22	17	19
5	20	16	14	10	25	15
6	15	20	14	19	17	16
7	19	19	22	10	15	17
TOTAL	115	128	112	112	122	118

Low numbers: 355   High numbers: 352

"With this information, what can we say about Natalya's question?" I asked.

"Look, 355 and 352 are close, so you get low numbers and high numbers about the same," Nathan offered.

"Any other thoughts?" I asked.

"We rolled 3s the same as the 4s, and 3 is a low number and 4 is a high number," Kim noticed.

"How many of you agree that when you roll one die, sometimes you get low numbers and sometimes you get high numbers?" I asked. All hands went up.

"If I roll a die again, will I roll a low number or a high number?" I asked. There was a chorus of highs and lows.

"You all sound sure about what I would roll. Are you sure or are you just guessing?" I asked.

"You have to guess," Cecilia said. "You can't be sure."

I then wrote on the board:

When you roll one die, it is likely that _____.
When you roll one die, it is unlikely that _____.

"Talk to your partner about how you could complete these sentences," I said. I gave the children a few minutes to talk to one another, and then I asked for their ideas.

"I know one for unlikely," Kirk said.

"Okay," I said.

"It is unlikely that I will always get a 6," he said.

"Any other ideas?" I asked.

"It is likely that some numbers will be high and some will be low," Luisa said.

"It is unlikely to roll the same number all the time," Mitch said.

"It is not likely you will roll the number you want," Kim added.

The notion that some events are equally likely to occur is an important one in the study of probability. Another important notion is that sets of experimental data do not always match the theoretical probability. To focus the class on these ideas, I said, "Mathematicians would say that when you roll one die, all numbers are equally likely." I added *equally likely* to the Probability Words chart.

I asked the children to look at the class results for each of the numbers.

"These totals aren't all exactly the same," I noted. "Right now, the number 2 came up more than any other number, but if we added more data, chances are that 2 wouldn't still be in the lead. All of the numbers have an equally likely chance of coming up, and the totals should stay pretty even."

I knew that this idea was too abstract for many of the children. With more time, however, and more experiences like this one, they would begin to think about the theoretical probabilities.

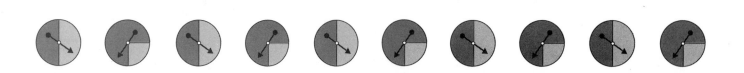

ASSESSMENT Likely and Unlikely

One of the important ideas in this unit is that some events are more likely to happen than others. Throughout the unit, students talk about the likelihood of events in their own lives and with cards, dice, and spinners. This assessment asks children to explain what the words *likely* and *unlikely* mean and to illustrate their explanations with examples. This assessment is appropriate about halfway through the unit, after students have had experience working on several menu activities, including *Likely–Unlikely Book*. (See page 94.)

Before having the children write, you might want to review with the class the probability terminology introduced so far. Ask students to explain some of the terms on the Probability Words chart and to give examples of how these can be used. Then have children write individually about what *likely* and *unlikely* mean and give examples. To help them get started working, write a prompt on the board for them to use if they'd like:

> Likely means _____.
> Unlikely means _____.
> Give examples.

FROM THE CLASSROOM

About two weeks after we started the probability unit, I asked the class to review the words on our Probability Words chart.

I began, "When we talked about the words weather reporters use, Nathan gave an example. He said, 'There's an 80 percent chance of rain today.' What kind of a chance is an 80 percent chance?"

"It's a pretty good chance," Matt offered.

"It's almost completely likely," Rachel said.

"What percent would be completely likely?" I asked, purposely using Rachel's terminology.

"One hundred percent would be for sure," Juliette said.

"If two things are equally likely, what chance do you think each would have?" I continued.

"It's half and half," Timothy suggested.

"I think it would be 50 percent," Cindy said with uncertainty.

"Yes," I said. "If two events are equally likely, each has a 50 percent chance of happening and 50 percent chance of not happening."

"Our spinners were 50-50," Cecilia remembered. "They were half red and half blue."

"That's right," I said.

"What about *possible* and *impossible?*" I then asked. "Can someone give an example of something that is possible or impossible to happen?"

"It's impossible for us to turn into frogs," Anne-Marie giggled.

"It's possible for tadpoles to turn into frogs," Chris said.

"What about likely and unlikely?" I asked.

"Some things are likely and some things are unlikely," Natalya said.

"Give an example," I said.

"It's likely we'll finish our menu," Lea said.

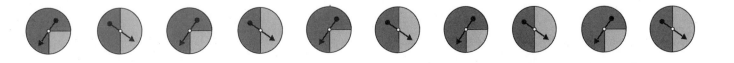

"It's unlikely we'll have an earthquake," Matt said.

I then introduced the assessment. "I'm very interested in knowing how each of you would explain what *likely* and *unlikely* mean," I said. "The more I know about how each of you thinks, the better I can help you learn."

I wrote on the board:

Likely means _____.
Unlikely means _____.
Give examples.

The Children's Writing

I read the children's work to see who understood what *likely* and *unlikely* meant and what sorts of examples the children gave to illustrate their understanding. Some papers were complete and correct. Luisa, for example, wrote: *Likely means it is probably going to happen. Unlikely means its probably not going to happen. Here's two examples. It is likely that I will roll a one two times in a row. It is unlikely that I can roll 1,000,000 1's in a row.*

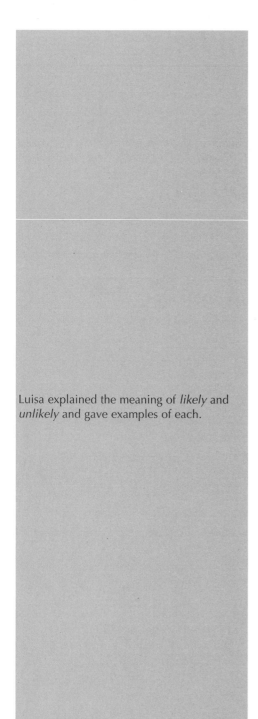

Luisa explained the meaning of *likely* and *unlikely* and gave examples of each.

> Likely means it is probably going to happen.
>
> Unlikely means its probably not going to happen.
>
> Here's two examples. It is likely that I will roll a one two times in a row.
>
> It is unlibley that I can roll 1000,000 1's in arow.

While some papers were incomplete, they indicated that the children understood the ideas. Yasmine , for example, explained what *likely* and *unlikely* meant but didn't include any examples. She wrote: *Likely means it has a good chanc of being what ever it was that you say is likely. Unlikely means it does not have a good chanc of being something.*

Nathan defined both words, then gave an example for *likely* but not for *unlikely*. He wrote: *Likely means it will most posaply happen. Unlikely means it will most not posaply happen. It is most likely blue has a better avantage of wining on the spinner. Its most likely red will not win on the spinner.*

Nathan drew a spinner to illustrate his likely example.

Likely means –
UnLikely means –

Likely means it will most posaply happen. UnLikely means it will most not posply happen.

It is most likely blue has a better avantage of wining on the spinner Its most likely red will not win on the spinner

blue
Red

Aaron also did not give examples. He wrote: *Likely means it might happen. unLikely means it might not happen.*

Aaron did not give examples to support his definitions.

Likely means it might happen

unLikely means it might not happen.

Lauren gave two lengthy explanations but included an example only for unlikely. She wrote: *Unlikely means we know it isen't going to happen. Likely means it will happen, but sometimes it doesn't happen. Unlikely means it won't happen but sometimes it does happen. It is Unlikely to get 8 six in a row in cards.*

Lauren clearly defined the two words but gave an example only of an unlikely event.

> Likely means we know it is going to happen.
> Unlikely means we know it isen't going to happen.
>
> Likely means it will happen, but sometimes it doesn't happen.
> Unlikely means it won't happen but sometimes it does happen.
>
> It is Unlikely to get 8 six in a row in cards

For several children, there was still some confusion about the term *unlikely*. For example, Cecilia's paper indicated that she thought *unlikely* meant *impossible*. She wrote: *Likely means it could happen. Unlikely means it can't happen. It is likely to roll one, two, three, four, five, and six when you use on die. It is unlikely to roll 15.* (For similar confusion, see page 142 of the assessment *When You Roll Two Dice.*)

Cecilia confused *unlikely* with *impossible*.

> Likely means it could happen.
> Unlikely means it can't happen.
>
> It is likely to roll one, two, three, four, five, and six when you use on die
>
> It is unlikely to roll 15.

The children's misconceptions and partial understanding were not surprising to me. I expect confusion when children are learning new ideas. I planned to continue to talk about these words and to use them in the contexts of the probability activities during the remainder of the unit.

MENU ACTIVITY

Overview

More Spinners

In *More Spinners,* students repeat the experience they had with the whole class lesson *Spinner Experiment* (see page 46), but they use spinners that are $\frac{1}{4}$ red and $\frac{3}{4}$ blue. They predict what will happen when they spin the spinner, then they do the experiment, and later they write about their results. The activity not only gives children experience with a spinner for which the outcomes are not equally likely but also introduces children to the fractional language of fourths and quarters. The assessment *100 Spins* (see page 127) relates to this menu activity and leads into the homework assignment *Spinners.* (See page 165.)

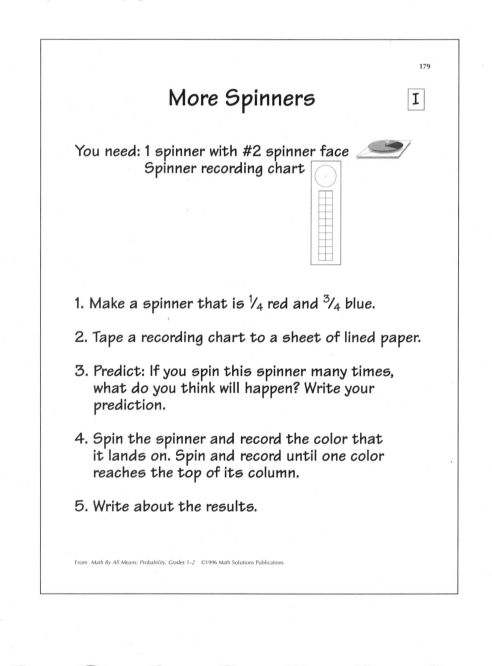

179

More Spinners I

You need: 1 spinner with #2 spinner face
Spinner recording chart

1. Make a spinner that is $\frac{1}{4}$ red and $\frac{3}{4}$ blue.

2. Tape a recording chart to a sheet of lined paper.

3. Predict: If you spin this spinner many times, what do you think will happen? Write your prediction.

4. Spin the spinner and record the color that it lands on. Spin and record until one color reaches the top of its column.

5. Write about the results.

From *Math By All Means: Probability, Grades 1–2* ©1996 Math Solutions Publications

Before the lesson

Gather these materials:
- Spinner Faces #2, one per student (See Blackline Masters section, page 177.) (Use a compass point to poke a hole in the center of each spinner face.)
- One Spinner Face #2 with lines drawn to divide it into fourths
- 5-by-8-inch index cards, one per pair of students (Cut each one in half so each student gets a 5-by-4-inch card. Use a compass point to poke a hole near the center of each piece.)
- Paper clips, one per child (Pull up one end of each paper clip so that it is perpendicular to the rest of the paper clip.)

- Plastic straws, one $1/4$-inch length per child
- Scissors
- Tape
- How to Make a Spinner, copies as needed for students (See Blackline Masters section, page 175.)
- Spinner recording charts, one per student (See Blackline Masters section, page 178.)
- Post-it Notes ($1\frac{1}{2}$ by 2 inches), one pad
- Red and blue markers or crayons, one of each color per student
- Blackline master of menu activity, page 179

Getting started

■ Tell students that they will make a spinner that is a little different from the one they made for the earlier spinner lesson. Hold up a cut-out Spinner Face #2 on which you drew lines to divide it into fourths.

■ Ask the children how many sections are on the spinner face. Introduce the terminology for one-fourth and one-quarter.

■ Color $1/4$ of the spinner face red. Reinforce for the children that the red section is called one-fourth or one-quarter.

■ Color one of the remaining quarters blue and ask the children what color they think the spinner will land on if they spin it. Continue, coloring another quarter blue and then the last quarter, until you have a spinner face that is $1/4$ red and $3/4$ blue. Introduce the terminology for three-fourths and three-quarters.

■ Using the spinner face, demonstrate how to make the spinner. (See the illustrated spinner assembly directions on page 47.)

■ Read the menu directions with the children and show them the materials they need. Demonstrate how the students are to prepare their papers by taping a recording chart to the left side of a sheet of lined paper, then writing the title, their name, and their prediction on the paper.

■ Ask a student to spin the spinner while you color in squares on the recording chart with blue and red marking pens. Remind the class to stop when one color reaches the top of the recording chart and then write about the results.

■ Encourage students to help one another make the spinners. If needed, provide copies of the blackline master How to Make a Spinner (see page 175) for review.

FROM THE CLASSROOM

I told the children that for this task they would make spinners similar to the ones they had made for the *Spinner Experiment* lesson. I held up a sample of the spinner face on which I had drawn lines to divide it into fourths.

"How many sections does this spinner face have?" I asked, to focus the children on the new spinner face.

"Four," several students said in unison.

"What do we call one of the four sections?" I asked, to see if any of the children knew fraction terminology. No one had an idea, so I explained, "The spinner is divided into four sections that are each the same size. We call each section one-fourth or one-quarter." Then, pointing to each section, I said, "So it's one-fourth, one-fourth, one-fourth, and one-fourth. Or, you could say, one-quarter, one-quarter, one-quarter, one-quarter."

I wrote $\frac{1}{4}$ on the board. "That means 1 out of 4 parts," I said, pointing to the fraction I had written.

I colored one section red and asked, "How much of this spinner face is red?"

A few children answered with "One-fourth" or "One-quarter," and I repeated for them, "It's one of four sections, so it's called one-fourth or one-quarter."

I then colored one section blue and asked, "If we spin this spinner now, what do you think will happen?"

"Red and blue are equal," Dylan said.

"What do you think will happen when you spin the spinner? What color will come up?" I asked.

"Maybe blue, maybe red," Luisa offered.

"White would win," Kirk said. "That's the biggest."

"What if I color another quarter blue?" I asked, as I colored in another fourth of the spinner face.

"Blue would probably win," Jack said. Several children agreed.

"Why?" I asked.

"Because blue has the biggest space," Aquilina said.

I colored the remaining quarter blue and asked, "Now what color do you think the spinner is most likely to land on?"

"Blue is going to win," Cecilia said.

"I think red will win because when you want something to happen it doesn't always happen," Juliette told us.

"If one-fourth of the spinner is red, what part is blue?" I asked.

"Three one-fourths are blue," Lea said.

"Yes, three-fourths are blue," I said. I pointed as I explained, "One-fourth, one-fourth, and one-fourth make three-fourths altogether." I wrote on the board:

$$\frac{1}{4} + \frac{1}{4} + \frac{1}{4} = \frac{3}{4}$$

As before, I didn't discuss the notation.

"Each of you will make a spinner that is one-fourth red and three-fourths blue. Watch as I make a spinner just as we did before. Follow closely, and see if you remember how to make it." I made the spinner while the class watched.

"Can we work with a partner?" Natalya asked.

"You may help one another, but you each need to make your own spinner," I responded. "Yours won't have lines dividing the face into fourths, but you'll still color it one-fourth red and three-fourths blue." I held up one of the spinner faces they would use.

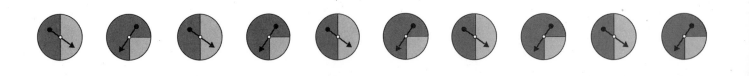

When I completed making my spinner, I said, "Once your spinner is ready, you'll also need a recording chart and a sheet of paper." I held up a recording chart. "Remember this recording chart? It's the same one you used in the other spinner experiment. You'll need to tape it to the left side of a sheet of lined paper, like this. Then put the name of the activity on the top of your paper along with your name." I demonstrated as I gave directions.

"Let's look at the directions," I said. I pointed to the enlarged menu task I had posted. "I already did steps 1 and 2." I read these to the children.

"What do you do next?" I asked Jack to read number 3 on the enlarged task.

He read, "Predict: If you spin this spinner many times, what do you think will happen? Write your prediction."

"So, the next thing you do is make a prediction," I said as I wrote the word *prediction* on the sample paper. "What next?"

"Spin the spinner and record the color that it lands on. Spin and record until one color reaches the top of its column," Cindy read.

I asked Dean to spin my spinner as I used red and blue marking pens to color in the squares on the recording chart.

"Be sure to stop when one color reaches the top," I emphasized, as I colored in the last blue square.

I didn't have the class use cubes to collect the data for this second spinner activity because I did not plan to collect the class data in the same way we did for the whole class lesson *Spinner Experiment*. Since children would be doing this activity at different times and on different days, the logistics of keeping track of the cubes that represented individual data seemed too cumbersome.

"Next it says to write about the results," I said. "How could we describe these results?" I asked.

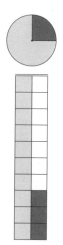

"Blue won," Mitch said.

"I knew blue would win," Rachel said.

"What else could you say to describe the results?" I asked.

"Blue got 10 and red only had 3," Davy reported.

"Blue beat red by 7 squares," Mario added.

"Underneath your prediction, write about what happened in your experiment," I said.

I colored in the square for *More Spinners* on the menu list, indicating that this activity was now a choice during menu time.

Observing the Children

Many children made the spinner the same day I introduced the activity, curious to know the results of the spinning. The class was active, as children went to get materials. Some went to get their menu folders, others picked up scissors, still others gathered the spinner materials that were set out on the supply table. Children often conferred with their partners, saying things such as "You get the folder, and I'll get the paper." Others just worked on their own. Before long, things settled down and everyone was involved with a menu task.

I noticed that Chris was busy coloring his spinner while Juliette, sitting next to him, looked a little lost. As I came close to their table, Juliette said, "I was absent when you made the other spinner."

"If you're not sure about how to make your spinner, what can you do?" I asked.

"Ask someone?" she responded in a questioning tone.

"That's right," I said. "I see other children making spinners right now. Chris seems to know how to make a spinner; you could ask him."

I could have asked Chris to help Juliette. Encouraging children to help one another had been a major focus all year long. But I also want children to learn how to ask for help. I moved on, hoping that if I left the scene, Juliette would be comfortable asking for help.

Kim came up to me holding her spinner and looking upset. "What's the problem?" I asked.

"My spinner's messed up," she said, showing me that it didn't spin properly.

Kim had managed to twist the paper clip into an unrecognizable form and had made the hole in the spinner face so large that you could have put your finger through it. This situation made me remember why I had taken the time to prepare the paper clips and to poke the holes in the spinner faces and cards. I suggested that she get a new spinner face and paper clip.

"I'll open the paper clip for you," I told her. "Then if you need help, ask someone who has finished making a spinner."

I continued around the room checking on how others were doing. Lea had prepared her spinner and spinner paper. She had very neatly written *prediction* on her paper and was now busy spinning and coloring in the recording chart. I interrupted her.

"Before you spin again," I said, "what color do you think the spinner will land on most?"

"Blue," she said.

NOTE Children need to be encouraged and reminded that they can get help from others. Some children are shy, some are hesitant to admit they don't know something, and still others aren't sure they're allowed to ask for help.

"Why do you think that?" I asked.

"There's more blue?" she responded, unsure.

"Write your prediction and reason on your paper before you do any more spinning," I told her. "This way you'll be able to test your prediction."

"Oh," she said, and began to write.

Cindy, seated next to Lea, was spinning and coloring. She had predicted that red would win and it was, according to her recording sheet. I watched as she spun her spinner very gently, barely getting her spinner to move so that it would land on red once again.

"May I try your spinner?" I asked. Cindy passed her spinner to me. I gave it a good spin, and it landed on blue.

"You need to give it a good spin each time and let the spinner decide what color to land on," I said. "That will make it a more fair mathematical experiment."

By the time I reached Matt and Wade, they had completed their spinning and recording.

"We finished," Wade told me.

"Blue won on both of ours," Matt added.

"You've done a good job so far," I commented, "but there's something you haven't done yet. Go look at the directions for this activity, and see if you can figure out what else you need to do."

I often find that children hurry to complete a menu task but neglect the final direction. Often it's the part that asks them to write or reflect on their findings. In this case, it was the part that asked them for a prediction—the part that would give me some information about their thinking.

A Class Discussion

At the beginning of class the next week, I told the children to complete their spinner experiments so we could talk about the results by the end of math time.

Near the end of the math period, I asked the children to put away their materials and put their *More Spinners* papers on their desks. When all were ready, I asked, "What did you find out from this spinner experiment?" I called on Aaron.

"Blue won when I did it," he said.

"How many of you had blue win?" I asked. Most hands went up.

"Keep your hands up so I can count," I told them. There were 21 hands. I wrote on the board:

Blue   21

"How many had red win?" I asked. Six children raised their hands. I wrote:

Red   6

"How many of you predicted that blue would win?" I asked next. All but three children raised their hands.

> **NOTE** Some first and second grade children already have the idea that the main purpose of a classroom activity is to get it done. As teachers, we need to work hard to change this perception and help them learn that thinking about what they've done is important to their learning.

"So most of you predicted blue, and blue did win most," I said.

"I predicted blue, but red won on mine," Kim said.

"Me, too," Brian said.

Several hands went up. Other students wanted to talk about their predictions, but I wanted to take the emphasis off whether or not they had predicted correctly, so I asked, "Why did so many of you predict that blue would win?"

"Red is only a small piece," Yasmine said.

"Blue is the biggest," Matt told us.

"What do we call the part of the circle that's colored red?" I asked. "There is a fraction name for it."

"It's a fourth," Rachel said.

"What about the blue part?" I asked next.

"Three-fourths," Nathan remembered.

The Children's Writing

When reviewing children's predictions for the new spinner, I found that many students understood that their predictions needed to be based on the amount of space each color had on the spinner. For example, Lea wrote: *I think blue will win because blue takes up more of the spinner.*

To Lea it was clear that blue would win because it took up more of the spinner.

Spinner

prediction I think blue will win because blue takes up more of the spinner

results
Blue won by nine.
Red lost by nine

Kim wrote: *I think that blue will win because three are blue and oney one is red.* The spinner face on her chart was less than one-fourth red. It's difficult for some young children to draw fourths accurately.

Kim's prediction noted that three sections of the spinner were blue and one was red.

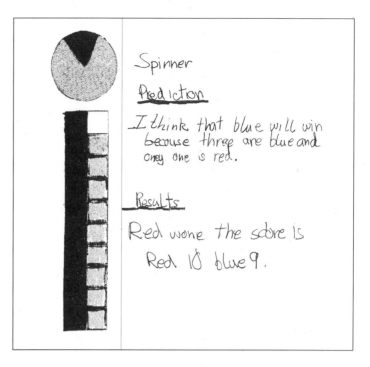

A few students used fractional terminology in their predictions. For example, Natalya wrote: *I think that blue will win because it has 3 4ths and red has 1 4th.*

Natalya used fractional notation in her prediction.

Other students were still struggling to make sense of fractions. Fredric colored his spinner as Kim had, showing red as only about one-eighth of the spinner. For his prediction, he wrote: *blue because there are more blue on the spinner and there are 1 half of red.*

Fractional parts were still new and unclear to Fredric.

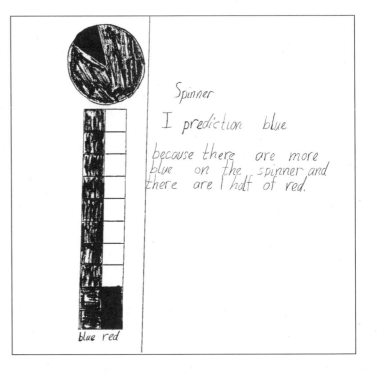

Spinner

I prediction blue

because there are more blue on the spinner and there are 1 half of red.

blue red

NOTE Confusion with terminology and notation is typical for children this age. When learning something new, students need to hear correct language and see correct notation used in contexts. This probability experiment provides students with the opportunity to learn about the fractional language and notation of fourths and quarters.

Some students' predictions didn't refer to the colored sections of the spinner at all. For example, Dylan wrote: *I think blue will win because it has a better chance.*

This activity was some students' first introduction to fractions. By first and second grade, children have often heard references to some common fractions. Some children may even have the correct idea about what $\frac{1}{2}$ or $\frac{1}{4}$ means. But most children at this age haven't heard fractional terminology, seen the numerical symbolization for fractions, or had practice sketching fractional parts. This probability experiment provides an introductory experience with the idea of fourths.

ASSESSMENT 100 Spins

FROM THE CLASSROOM

The menu task *More Spinners* (see page 117) asks students to make a second spinner, predict what will happen when they spin it, and test their predictions by collecting a small sample of data. During the class discussion, students pool their data and interpret a larger sample. This assessment asks children to use this information to predict in a new situation. This is a time for them to extend their thinking and for the teacher to learn about their ability to apply what they have learned to a hypothetical experiment. It also gives the teacher an opportunity to find out about individual students' notions of probability, number sense, and communication skills.

This assessment is appropriate after students have done and discussed the menu activity *More Spinners.* To introduce the assessment, show students the spinner that is one-fourth red and three-fourths blue from the *More Spinners* activity. Review the data that the class collected. Then ask students to predict what would happen if they were to spin the spinner 100 times, to write their predictions on Post-it Notes, and to put them on the board. Discuss the various predictions, then ask the students to write their predictions on their *More Spinners* papers.

After this assessment, assign the *Spinners* homework assignment. (See page 165.) In that assignment, students spin their spinners with someone at home, then return to class to compile their data and test their predictions.

I held up one of the spinners the children had made for *More Spinners* and said, "When you worked on the menu activity, you made a spinner that was one-fourth red and three-fourths blue. Then you predicted what color the spinner would land on. Now I'd like you to make another prediction. If you were to spin your spinner 100 times, how many times do you think it would come up blue and how many times red?"

Students immediately offered predictions. "It'll be blue for sure." "Mostly blue—more than half." "I think 90 blue."

"I want each of you to write on a Post-it how many spins you think would be blue and how many would be red. You don't have to put your name on this prediction."

I wrote on the board:

> ___ blue
> ___ red

"When your prediction is ready, put your Post-it on the board and have a seat on the rug," I said.

I quickly distributed Post-its, and the children began writing their predictions. Once all had posted their predictions and were seated, I asked, "What could we do to organize our predictions?" The Post-its were scattered randomly on the blackboard.

"Some are the same," Cecilia noticed.

I asked Cecilia to help find the ones that were the same. All of the predictions except 75 blue, 25 red and 76 blue, 26 red had at least one

duplicate. Once they were grouped by like predictions, I asked if there was anything else we could do to make the information easier to discuss.

"We could find all the ones that thought blue would win," Chris suggested.

We followed Chris's suggestion and found that everyone had predicted blue would win, except for two students who thought the results would be 50 blue and 50 red.

"We could put the numbers in order," Brian offered.

"How would you start?" I asked.

"With the biggest," he quickly answered.

I asked Kirk and Lea to put the Post-its in order. They did this easily until they came to one Post-it that said 76 blue and 26 red.

"What's the problem?" I asked.

"This one doesn't add up to 100," Kirk reported.

"What do you think it should be?" I asked.

"Probably 75 and 25," he said, adding it to that group.

The results looked like this:

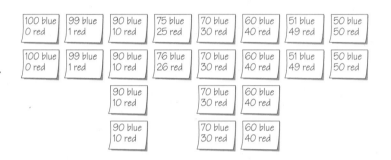

"When you examine all of our predictions, what can you say about what our class thinks will happen when you spin 100 times?" I asked.

"Most think blue will win for sure," Natalya said.

"Blue will probably get 60, 70, or 90," Timothy added.

"Can we spin 100 times?" Lea asked, eager to try it.

"Later today I'll give you the homework assignment to collect data to find out what happens when you spin 100 times," I said. "For now, I'd like you to take out your *More Spinners* papers and write a prediction on it." I wrote on the board:

If we spin 100 times, _____.

The Children's Predictions

Some students seemed to look at their own experiences to make their predictions. For example, when Juliette did *More Spinners,* blue came up 10 times and red came up 9. Her prediction was: *If I rolled 100 times It woud end up 49 51.*

Luisa also based her prediction on her own sample. On her recording sheet, blue had 10 and red had 0. She later predicted: *If we spin 100 times we think it is blue becaus it has the most color, and blue will win and red lose. 100 blue and 0 red.*

Juliette's prediction of 49 and 51 seemed to be based on the results from her experiment.

Spinner

Prediction I think blue will win becouse it has a better cance

results bule won by one

If I rolled 100 times It woud end up 49 51

Chris's recording sheet showed that his spinner had landed on red 3 times and blue 10 times. He wrote: *If I spin 100 times I think blue would win because it has more qurts* [quarters] *than red. I think it will be 10 reds and 90 blues.*

When Fredric did *More Spinners,* red won by 1 spin. He predicted, however, that blue would win in 100 spins. He wrote: *If we spin 100 times we think that blue will win. I think blue will have 60 and red will have 40.*

Fredric predicted that the spinner would land on blue 60 times and on red 40 times.

Spinner

We think that blue will win

Red won

If we spin 100 times we think that blue will win. I think blue will have 60 and red will have 40.

Mario's prediction for *More Spinners* was that blue would win—and it did—but he predicted a 50-50 split for 100 spins.

On Mario's paper, blue came up 10 times and red came up 4 times. Yet he wrote: *If we spin 100 times I think it will be a tie and I thint the scores will be 50 50.*

Brian had trouble making any kind of prediction.

Brian didn't make a numerical prediction. He wrote: *If I spin 100 time ill be a lot of spins.*

Cecilia mentioned the fraction ¹/₄ in her prediction.

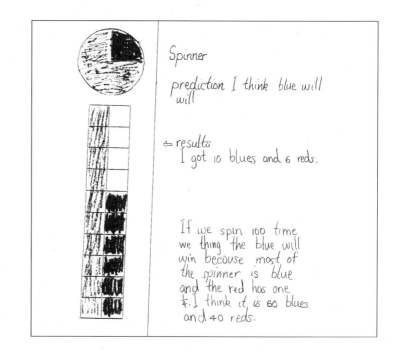

Spinner

prediction I think blue will
will

⇐ results
I got 10 blues and 6 reds.

If we spin 100 time
we thing the blue will
win becouse most of
the spinner is blue
and the red has one
¼. I think it is 80 blues
and 40 reds.

At these grade levels, I expect children to predict that blue will win with 100 spins. However, I don't expect their numerical predictions to reflect exactly the proportions of the red and blue parts of the spinner. When I read each paper, I look to see if the prediction is reasonable.

MENU ACTIVITY

Overview

Roll Two Dice

In this activity, students practice basic addition facts as they roll two dice and keep track of the combinations that come up. They continue until one sum fills a column on a recording sheet. Students post the winning sums on a class chart and later discuss the reasons why some sums are more likely to come up than others.

In the related homework assignment (see page 166), students teach the game to someone at home, play at least one game, then add their results to the class chart and discuss the data. Also, the assessment *When You Roll Two Dice* (see page 140) continues the discussion and asks children to write about what happens when they roll two dice.

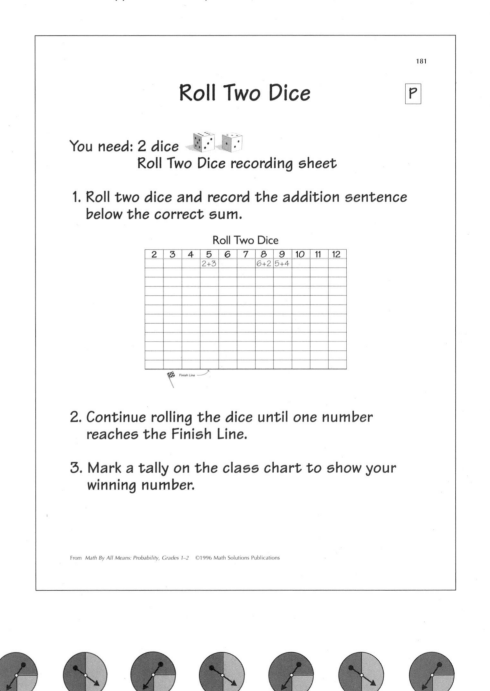

181

Roll Two Dice [P]

You need: 2 dice
        Roll Two Dice recording sheet

1. Roll two dice and record the addition sentence below the correct sum.

Roll Two Dice

2	3	4	5	6	7	8	9	10	11	12
			2+3			6+2	5+4			

Finish Line

2. Continue rolling the dice until one number reaches the Finish Line.

3. Mark a tally on the class chart to show your winning number.

From *Math By All Means: Probability, Grades 1–2* ©1996 Math Solutions Publications

Before the lesson

Gather these materials:
- ■ *Roll Two Dice* recording sheets, one per pair of students (See the Blackline Masters section, page 182.)
- ■ Dice, two per pair of students
- ■ One sheet of chart paper, titled "Roll Two Dice" and listing the numbers from 2 to 12 down the left side.
- ■ Blackline master of menu activity, page 181

Getting started

■ Talk with the students about the outcomes that are possible when they roll two dice. Begin by asking students what are the lowest and highest sums they can get with two dice. Then ask if all the sums between 2 and 12 are also possible. Have the children think about this in pairs.

■ Ask the students to report ways they can make sums from 2 to 12 by rolling two dice. Record on the board what they report. Continue until you've recorded at least one way to make each sum.

■ Review the menu directions and show the children the *Roll Two Dice* recording sheet. Explain that, working in pairs, they will roll two dice and record addition sentences for the two numbers that come up. Demonstrate how to write each addition sentence in the correct column on the recording sheet.

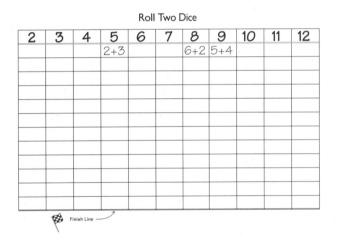

■ Tell the students that they should keep rolling the dice and recording addition sentences until one column reaches the "Finish Line" on the recording sheet.

■ Post the class chart titled "Roll Two Dice." Explain to the students that when they complete a *Roll Two Dice* recording sheet, they should put a tally mark next to the sum that filled its column.

```
┌─────────────────────────────┐
│        Roll Two Dice        │
│                             │
│   2                         │
│   3                         │
│   4                         │
│   5                         │
│   6                         │
│   7                         │
│   8                         │
│   9                         │
│   10                        │
│   11                        │
│   12                        │
│                             │
│                             │
└─────────────────────────────┘
```

■ Tell the students to repeat the activity several times.

■ After students have had several days to work on this activity, initiate a discussion by asking the children to compare the results of this investigation with the results from *Roll One Die.*

FROM THE CLASSROOM

NOTE Sometimes a class discussion moves into a different direction or takes longer than the teacher planned. Deciding when to end a discussion and when to let it run its course varies in each situation.

Before posting the directions for this activity, I asked the class, "When you roll two dice and add the numbers that come up, what's the lowest sum that you can get?" Several hands went up, and I called on Kim.

"You can get a 1," she said.

"I agree that you can get a 1 when you roll one die," I said, "but what if you roll two dice?"

"You can roll two 1s and that makes 2," said Kirk, being specific.

"What's the highest sum possible with two dice?" I asked.

"Twelve," Timothy answered.

"So, we know we can get sums of 2 and 12. What about the other numbers in between?" I wondered aloud. "Talk to the person next to you and see what other sums you think are possible with two dice."

Everyone seemed involved in discussing this problem. Some children got out pencil and paper, while others went to get dice. What I had intended to be a brief discussion had now turned into a major investigation. I decided to give the students time to satisfy their curiosity. Some of the children not only investigated what sums were possible but also how many ways they could get each one.

After about five minutes, I called for the students' attention. I asked them to put down their pencils and place the dice in the center of their tables.

"I'm going to call on different people to report one possible sum and one way to get that sum using two dice," I told them.

I listed the numbers on the board as children reported them.

"You could get a 3 and a 3," Yasmine reported.

"What sum would that be?" I asked.

"Six," she said.

As I recorded her example on the board, I asked, "Is there another way to get the sum of 6 using two dice?"

"A 4 and a 2," Cindy said quietly.

"What about 5 and 1?" Chris added.

"Any others?" I asked. No one raised a hand.

"I know a way to get 11," Natalya offered.

I wrote *11* on the board, and Natalya added, "It's 5 plus 6."

I continued listing the numbers on the board as children reported them. When the students thought that all possible sums were listed, I asked, "Are any sums between 2 and 12 impossible?" Because they had reported the numbers in random order, it took them a while to check.

"I think they're all possible," said Mario. He came to the board. "See, here's one way to make a 3, then 4, 5, 6, 7, 8, 9, 10, and 11." He pointed to each number as he found it on the list. His own paper was more systematic than the list on the board.

I then posted on the board the enlarged directions for *Roll Two Dice* and taped a recording sheet alongside. I asked the class to look at the menu directions. We quickly reviewed the materials needed and noted that this was a partner activity. I told the children that each time they rolled the dice they should write the two numbers that came up as an addition sentence below the correct sum.

I modeled on the recording sheet how to record. I rolled the dice and got a 2 and a 3. Below the 5 on the recording sheet, I wrote *2 + 3*. On the following rolls, a 6 and a 2 and a 5 and a 4 came up. I wrote these sums in their columns.

Roll Two Dice

2	3	4	5	6	7	8	9	10	11	12
			2+3			6+2	5+4			

Finish Line ⟶

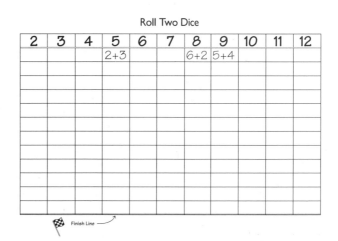

Then I asked, "What do you think we're trying to find out from this activity?" I waited to give the children time to think, and then I called on Nathan.

"We want to see which number will win?" he said, tentatively.

"Yes," I said, "and we also want to find out if some sums are more likely to come up than others. When you fill the column for one sum, stop and put a tally mark on the class chart next to that number." I posted the chart I had titled "Roll Two Dice."

"We'll talk about the results when everyone has completed the task," I concluded. "Do this activity several times so that we'll have a lot of data on our chart."

Observing the Children

Most of the pairs of children who chose this activity quickly settled into a smooth working relationship. Some pairs took turns rolling the dice and writing; other pairs seemed happy with one person rolling the dice while the other did all of the recording.

There were still a few students, however, who hadn't quite learned how to work together. Timothy, for example, asked, "Do we have to do this with a partner?"

"Why do you think I asked you to do this activity with a partner?" I answered with a question.

"So we can help each other," he responded quite easily.

"Why else?" I pushed.

Timothy couldn't think of another reason, so I gave additional rationales. "I think that it's important that you learn to work with each other," I said, "and also it's important that you have a partner to talk about what you're doing and what you're finding out.

"I notice that Dylan and Aaron have found a way to work together," I added, nodding at the two boys across the table. "Let's find out how

NOTE Creating a community where all children work together in helpful ways is an ongoing process. Children must understand why they are asked to work together. They also benefit from seeing and hearing how other children have learned to help each other.

they're doing it." I interrupted the boys and asked, "How are you two sharing the jobs for *Roll Two Dice?*"

"One of us rolls five times, and the other person writes. Then we take turns," Dylan said.

"You may want to work the way Aaron and Dylan are working, or you may want to choose your own way," I told Timothy and his partner, Nathan. "I'm sure you can find a way to work together."

I moved on to see how others were doing and watched Juliette and Megan take turns and easily write the number sentences in the proper columns. I knew that both girls knew most of the basic addition facts and decided to challenge their thinking beyond the collection of data.

"I wonder why you're getting so many 7s and 8s and no 2s or 12s," I mused, looking at their paper.

"Snake eyes are hard to get," Megan responded quickly.

"So is 6 and 6," Juliette added.

"All doubles are hard to get," Megan said.

"Have you rolled any doubles?" I asked. They examined their recording sheet and found that they had 2 + 2, 3 + 3, 4 + 4, and 5 + 5, each once.

"Not rolling doubles may be part of the reason why you rolled so many 7s and 8s and no 2s or 12s, but there may be other explanations," I said. "See if you can think about other reasons."

Juliette and Megan didn't roll any 2s, 3s, or 12s.

Roll Two Dice

2	3	4	5	6	7	8	9	10	11	12
		2+2	4+1	1+5	3+4	5+3	4+5	5+5	6+5	
			3+2	4+2	5+2	4+4	6+3	5+5	5+6	
			2+3	3+3	4+3	6+2	6+3	5+5	6+5	
				4+2	6+1	5+3	6+3			
					4+3	6+2	5+4			
					4+3	3+5	6+3			
					6+1		3+6			
					5+2					
					4+3					
					3+4					
					4+3					
					5+2					

Finish Line →

A Class Discussion

I began the math period one day by saying to the class, "When we looked at the data for *Roll One Die*, one of the things we noticed was that you couldn't tell for sure which number was going to win. Mathematicians say that when you roll one die, all numbers are equally likely. What do you think for *Roll Two Dice?* Are all sums equally likely?"

"No way," Kim said. Several students agreed with her.

"What can you say about the probabilities of the different sums from rolling two dice?" I asked.

"Some numbers are likely and some numbers are unlikely," Rachel said.

"What's another way you can say that?" I asked, wanting to hear from more children.

"Each number is not equally likely," Kirk offered.

"Why do you think some sums are more likely than others when you roll two dice?" I asked.

"Some are harder to get," Lea said.

"Why?" I probed.

"There's only one way to get 2 and only one way to get 12," Mario said. "You have to get doubles."

"What else?" I asked.

"There's lots of ways to get a 6," Fredric said. "You could roll a 4 and a 2, or 5 and 1, or 3 and 3."

"Let's think about rolling one die again," I said. "Why do mathematicians say that each number is equally likely when you roll one die?"

"When you just have one die, there's only one way to get a 6 and one way to get each number," Juliette said emphatically.

"There's only six numbers you can get with one die and way more for two dice," Cecilia said.

This was a promising discussion. The idea that there is a mathematical reason why some events are more likely than others is a sophisticated theoretical concept. Having children experiment with dice, discuss the results, and share their thinking provides valuable experience to connect later understanding. I didn't pursue the discussion further because I had planned an assessment in which the students would talk about the *Roll Two Dice* results and write about their thinking. (See page 140.)

Lea and Fredric rolled at least two of each sum in their game.

Roll Two Dice

2	3	4	5	6	7	8	9	10	11	12
1+1	2+1	3+1	3+2	4+2	6+1	3+5	5+4	6+4	6+5	6+6
1+1	2+1	2+2	3+2	1+5	3+4	3+5	6+3	6+4	6+5	6+6
	2+1		3+2	4+2	3+4	3+5	3+6	6+4	6+5	
	1+2		3+2		3+4	3+5	3+6	5+5		
	1+2		3+2		5+2	2+6	3+6	6+4		
	1+2				6+1	2+6	3+6			
					6+1	6+2				
						4+4				
						5+3				
						4+4				
						5+3				
						5+3				

Finish Line →

A Mathematical Note

When rolling two dice there are 36 possible ways to get the sums 2 through 12. For example, there are 5 ways to get the sum of 6: 3 + 3, 4 + 2, 2 + 4, 5 + 1, and 1 + 5. Reversed combinations count as two different ways to get a sum because they're actually different results with two dice. This idea can be shown by using dice of two different colors. For example, a 2 can come up on a red die and 4 on a blue die and vice versa. Doubles, however, cannot be reversed; the sum of 12 only has one way to come up, 6 on the red die and 6 on the blue one.

Sums from Two Dice

2	3	4	5	6	7	8	9	10	11	12
1+1	1+2	2+2	3+2	3+3	4+3	4+4	5+4	5+5	6+5	6+6
	2+1	3+1	2+3	4+2	5+3	4+5	6+4	5+6		
		1+3	4+1	2+4	6+1	3+5	6+3	4+6		
			1+4	5+1	1+6	6+2	3+6			
				1+5	5+2	2+6				
					2+5					

Total Ways										
1	2	3	4	5	6	5	4	3	2	1

ASSESSMENT When You Roll Two Dice

FROM THE CLASSROOM

Students bring to this assessment a good amount of experience with dice, both from the activities during this unit and prior experience with games at home and school. During the menu activity *Roll Two Dice*, students collected data to see whether some sums were more likely than others. This assessment provides the opportunity to gain insights into what the children now understand about the likelihood of sums from rolling two dice and how the class data influenced their thinking.

After a short class discussion about the results of *Roll Two Dice,* ask the children to write about what is likely and unlikely to happen when two dice are rolled.

I introduced this assessment by asking the class, "What do you know so far about rolling two dice?"

"I know that 5, 6, and 7 usually win," Mario said with certainty.

"Ten always wins when I roll dice," Yasmine reported.

"I always get 8," Lea said.

I directed the students' attention to the *Roll Two Dice* class chart. "First, let's look at the class chart to see what happened when you rolled two dice. Talk to the person sitting next to you about what you notice about the data on the chart and about which numbers are more likely to come up than others."

Roll Two Dice	
2	
3	
4	II
5	IIII I
6	IIII IIII II
7	IIII IIII III
8	IIII IIII IIII
9	III
10	
11	
12	

After a few minutes, I called on Luisa. "Eight is the easiest to get," she said.

"Who can explain what Luisa is thinking?" I asked.

"She means 8 got the most," Yasmine offered.

"And 6 and 7 came in second," Davy reported.

"They all came out different," Chris said.

"What do you mean?" I asked.

"There are 2 tally marks on 4, and 6 marks on 5, and 12 on 6, like that," he said.

"Five numbers never won," Aquilina offered, and then added, "They're 2, 3, 10, 11, and 12."

Several other children had their hands raised, but instead of continuing the discussion, I said, "I'm interested in knowing what each of you thinks, so I'd like you to write about your ideas."

I wrote on the board:

When you roll two dice, it is likely _____.
It is unlikely _____.

"Write about what you think is likely and what is unlikely to happen when you roll two dice," I said.

The children went right to work. When they completed their writing, they continued with their menu work.

When I examined the children's writing, I found that about half of the class had the idea that some sums were more likely than others. For example, Kirk wrote: *When you roll 2 dice it is likely that you will get a five or a six. It is unlikely that you will get a two or a twelve.*

Kirk believed that 5 or 6 were the most likely numbers.

Lea did not commit herself to identifying which sums were more or less likely. She wrote: *When you roll 2 dice It is likely you will roll 2 numbers. It is ulikely that you will pick a number and it will happen.*

Lea wrote a general comment about what was likely to occur.

Some of the children used the term *unlikely* to mean impossible. For example, Noelle wrote: *When you roll 2 dice It is likely that 10 will come up. It is unlikely 100 will come up.* Timothy wrote: *When you roll 2 dice It is likely that you mit get a six. It is unlikely that you get a 30 with two dice.*

Timothy used the word *unlikely* to mean impossible.

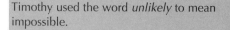

> When you roll 2 dice
> It is likely that you mit get a six.
>
> It is unlikely that you get a 30
> with two dice.

In her paper, Anne-Marie stated that the middle sums were more likely to come up than those at the beginning and end. This is correct, as 6, 7, and 8 are more likely than 2 or 12. However, Anne-Marie's example refers to rolling one die, not rolling two dice. Her paper is an indication of the partial understanding and confusion that often exist for children when they are learning something.

Anne-Marie's paper showed her partial understanding and her confusion.

> When you rol 2 dice
>
> It is likely that when you roll the
> dice you will get a three, because it is
> a middle number
>
> It is unlikely that you will get a 1 org
> 6, because it is a beginning number and
> a ending number.

Some of the children didn't address the mathematics at all. For example, Dean wrote: *It is likely that you roll two Dice. It is unlikely that you don't corwaperate with your partenr.*

I don't consider children who express erroneous ideas, or who don't address the mathematics, as being deficient. With all new ideas, learning develops over time and requires much experience and interaction. The probability of sums from rolling two dice is a complex idea. This assessment gave me insights into individual children's ideas and also into the range of how the children thought about the results of rolling two dice.

Dean didn't focus on the mathematical probabilities but instead on the activity.

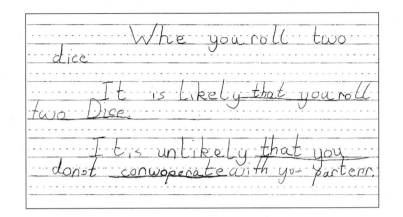

Whe you roll two dice

It is likely that you roll two Dice.

It is untikely that you don-t conwoperate with your partenr.

ASSESSMENT Agree or Disagree with Sara

FROM THE CLASSROOM

This assessment draws on students' experiences with rolling two dice, collecting data, and determining the likelihood of events. In this assignment, they examine whether it is more likely to roll two numbers that are the same or two numbers that are different.

Introduce the assessment by telling a story about two children who are trying to decide who will go first in a game. The first child suggests, "If you roll doubles, you can go first. If you don't roll doubles, I'll go first." The other child, Sara, responds by explaining, "It's unlikely that I'll get doubles, and it's likely that I'll get not doubles." (Note: In my class, I chose the name Sara. Choose a name not shared by a student in your class.)

Ask students, in pairs, to discuss and then write about whether they agree or disagree with Sara. Tell them that they need to provide some proof for their thinking by looking back at their *Roll Two Dice* recording sheets and by collecting more data from rolling dice again. Their papers will reveal whether they can organize data in a useful way and can draw conclusions from their data.

Early in the unit, I had a discussion with the children about some fair ways they knew to decide who would go first in a game or who would get the bigger of two cookies. They had suggested a variety of methods that they thought would work, and I was curious to see how they would respond to a new idea. I presented them with a hypothetical situation by telling them a story.

"Two children were trying to decide who would get to go first in a game," I began. "One suggested, 'You roll the dice. If you roll doubles, you can go first. If you don't roll doubles, I'll go first.'

"The other child, Sara, said, 'That's the likely, unlikely thing.'

"'What do you mean?' the first child asked.

"She explained, 'It's unlikely that I'll get doubles, and it's likely I'll get not doubles.'"

I wrote on the board:

> Sara thinks it is unlikely that she will get doubles.
> She thinks it is likely that she will get not doubles.

I then told the class, "You and your partner need to decide together whether you agree or disagree with Sara's statement and then write about your reasoning. Also, you need to have proof. You may want to look at your recording sheets from the *Roll Two Dice* menu activity, but you should also roll dice and collect more data to back up your thinking."

"Can we do more pages like we did for *Roll Two Dice?*" Ivy asked.

"No," I replied, "that recording sheet helped us look at the sums that came up. Think about some way to collect data so you can learn about doubles coming up."

For those who needed a start in their writing, I wrote a prompt on the board:

We rolled the dice to find if doubles are likely or unlikely.

All of the children got right to work. Some looked in their folders for their *Roll Two Dice* recording sheets. Others got dice and began to collect data.

I purposely didn't give the children a way to record, and in the beginning a few had trouble getting started. But when everyone had finished, we had many examples of how to collect results in an organized way. Some kept track of their results in two columns, one for doubles, and one for not doubles. To indicate what they rolled, some used tally marks, some drew pictures of the dice, and others listed the two numbers. Two pairs of students recorded only 10 samples, while another two pairs rolled the dice more than 100 times. Most students, however, collected between 20 and 60 samples.

After 30 minutes, when all had completed their papers, I had the children gather on the rug to report their results. Everyone agreed with Sara.

Dylan used the terms *same* (for doubles) and *different* (for not doubles). His data showed that he got doubles only once out of 30 rolls, and he wrote that there was a smaller chance of getting doubles. But his concluding sentence showed the fragility of his conviction. He wrote: *If you roll more times maybe you'll get more doubles.*

Dylan thought that if he rolled more times he might get more doubles.

Same or Different	
Same	Different
1	ⅢⅢ ⅢⅢ
	ⅢⅢ ⅢⅢ
	ⅢⅢ ⅢⅢ

The probability is the biggest chance is you'll get different numbers when you roll two dice. But you have a smaller chance of getting doubles. It is impossible to get doubles every time. If you roll more times maybe you'll get more doubles.

Mitch and Kim chose to draw pictures of the dice they rolled. They recorded only 11 samples, but their writing clearly communicated their findings. They wrote: *We got 3 that are doubles. We got eight dice that are not doubles. Yes, we agree with sarah that it is unlikely to get doubles.*

Mitch and Kim based their conclusions on a small sample.

We rolled the dice to find out if doubles are likely or unlikely. This is our results. We rolled 11 times. We got 3 that are doubles. We got eight dice that are not doubles. Yes, we agree with sarah that it is unlikely to get doubles.

Lea wrote on her paper: *We got five doubles and twenty four no doubles and Franklin agrees with me and we both agree with me and even Davy agreed with me.*

Rachel and Juliette drew tally marks to record whether each roll was a double or not. They organized their tallies into sets of 10. They wrote: *We rolled 53 not doubles and 16 doubles. We agree with Sara that doubles are unlikly.*

Rachel and Juliette drew tally marks to keep track of their rolls.

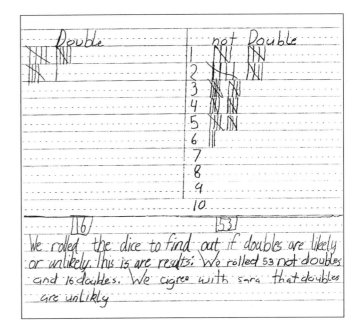

Holly and Megan wrote down what numbers came up on each roll and concluded that they agreed with Sara.

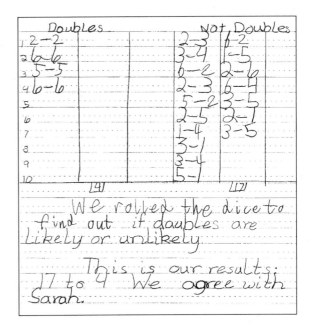

MENU ACTIVITY

The 1 to 10 Game

Overview

The 1 to 10 Game was invented by two second grade students during an earlier version of this probability unit. The game uses dice and cards and involves both strategy and chance. In this activity, children play the game many times, then discuss the strategies they used. The game sets the stage for a later menu activity in which the children invent their own games using cards and/or dice. (See page 153.) In a related homework assignment (see page 167), students teach someone at home to play *The 1 to 10 Game*, play several games, and think about strategies they used.

183

The 1 to 10 Game P

You need: Two dice

1 deck of cards ♠

1. Use only the ace, 2, 3, 4, 5, 6, 7, 8, 9, 10 cards.

2. One of you takes the red cards, and one of you takes the black cards.

3. Take turns. On your turn, roll the dice and figure out the sum. Remove enough cards from your hand to add up to that sum.

> For example, if you roll a 5 and a 3, you can make 8 in many ways, including:

4. If you can't make the sum with cards from your hand, roll again. If you can't make a sum after three rolls, you lose the game.

5. You win if your partner can't make a number in three rolls or if you use up all your cards.

From *Math By All Means: Probability, Grades 1–2* ©1996 Math Solutions Publications

Before the lesson

Gather these materials:
■ Dice, two per pair of students
■ Playing cards, one deck per pair of students
■ Blackline master of menu activity, page 183

Getting started

■ Post the directions and tell the class that *The 1 to 10 Game* was invented by two second grade children.

■ Choose a child to play a sample game with you. Have the students read the directions and watch as you play the game.

■ Hold up a deck of cards and remove the face cards so you have only ace to 10 for each of the four suits. Deal the remaining cards so that your partner has the 20 red cards and you have the 20 black cards.

■ Take turns rolling the dice, adding the numbers, and announcing the sum to the class. Then talk about the various combinations that can make that sum. Choose a combination and remove cards with those numbers from your hand. If you don't have cards that will work, roll again. Explain that if you can't make a sum in three rolls, you lose the game.

■ Tell the class that a person can win the game in either of two ways: by getting rid of all of the cards in his or her hand or if the partner can't make a sum in three rolls.

■ After the students play *The 1 to 10 Game* several times, initiate a class discussion. Ask whether the game involves chance, strategy, or both. Have the children describe the strategies they used.

FROM THE CLASSROOM

I began math class by having the children gather on the rug so I could teach them *The 1 to 10 Game.* I posted an enlarged version of the menu directions.

"Today we're going to learn a game that was invented by two second grade children," I told them once they were settled. "We'll read the directions and play a sample game, and then you'll have a chance to play it as part of the menu."

By the reaction of the children, I could tell that the idea that second graders could invent a game had captured their interest and awe.

"Do we get to invent a game, too?" asked Chris.

"In a few days, you'll get a chance to invent your own," I responded, "but right now our job is to learn this game." Several hands were up, and I called on Davy.

"I have a good idea for a game," he said eagerly.

"In a few days, you'll work with your partner to test your ideas and write your own directions for games," I repeated.

I referred the children to the task I had posted. "What's the name of the game we're going to play?" I asked.

"*The 1 to 10 Game,*" the children read in unison.

"Raise your hand if you know what materials you need to play this game," I continued. I called on Luisa.

"You need dice and cards," she said.

"What else do you need?" I asked. I saw some questioning looks.

"Do I play this game like solitaire?" I probed.

"You need a partner," said Mario.

"How does Mario know that?" I asked.

"There's a *P* on the directions," said Mitch.

I asked Aquilina to be my partner, and she joined me. "Now what do we do?" I asked.

"Take out the kings, queens, and jacks first," Natalya said.

"And maybe jokers, too," Nathan added.

I gave Aquilina some of the cards so she could help take out the cards we didn't need.

"Now what?" I asked, trying to involve the class in reading the directions.

"Give the red cards to Aquilina, and you get the black cards," Kirk said. I quickly sorted the cards.

"Now what?" I asked.

"Roll the dice," Chris said a bit impatiently. He's always anxious to get involved right away.

"You go first, Aquilina," I said. Aquilina rolled a 4 and a 5.

"Read the direction that gives an example of what Aquilina does next," I asked.

Rachel read: "Take turns. On your turn, roll the dice and figure out the sum. Remove enough cards from your hand to add up to that sum. For example, if you roll a 5 and a 3, you can make 8 in many ways, including . . . " Rachel looked at the pictures of the playing cards on the directions and continued, "5 and 3, 4 and 4, 4 and 2 and 2, or 8."

"What cards can Aquilina use with the numbers she rolled?" I asked.

"She could use a 4 and a 5," Cecilia replied.

"She could just use a 9," Cindy said.

"What else?" I asked.

"A 6 and a 3 or an 8 and a 1," Lea added.

"How can you make a 9 using three cards?" I asked.

"You could use a 2, a 3, and a 4," Matt suggested.

"So there are several ways for Aquilina to make 9," I said, and turned to Aquilina. "What are you going to do?" She decided to take out a 6 and a 3.

Then I rolled the dice. I rolled a 5 and a 1 and said aloud, "5 and 1 make 6, so I can take out a 6; or a 5 and a 1; or a 3 and a 3; or a 2 and a 4; or a 1, a 2, and a 3. I think I'll choose a 2 and a 4."

We continued the game, taking turns and involving the other children by playing our cards face up for all to see. When Aquilina rolled a 5 and a 3, she didn't have any cards left in her hand that added to 8.

"Now what do we do?" I asked.

We turned to the directions again and read step 4: "If you can't make the sum with cards from your hand, roll again. If you can't make a sum after three rolls, you lose the game."

"How do you win this game?" I asked.

"If your partner can't make a number," Cindy said.

"But they get to try three times," Nathan added, always paying attention.

"Is there another way to win?" I asked.

"If one of you runs out of cards before the other one does," Chris said after looking at the directions.

"So there are two ways to win," I said, "by using all of your cards or if your partner can't make a sum after three tries." After a few more turns, Aquilina had rolled the dice three times and still didn't have the cards she needed. I was declared the winner.

The 1 to 10 Game is one you should play many times," I told the class. "You may choose to play this new game now or continue with other activities on the menu."

Observing the Children

In a few minutes, the children were involved with various menu activities. As is typical when a new activity is introduced, *The 1 to 10 Game* was a popular choice.

Luisa brought the cards back to her table and began to sort out the face cards. Her partner Davy tried to grab the cards away from her. She complained.

I know that Luisa is quick and competent and needs to be reminded to give others a chance to be included. It's good that Davy wouldn't let her take over, but I wanted him to consider a way to protest other than grabbing.

"Why do you think Davy wants the cards?" I asked Luisa. She shrugged.

"Maybe Davy can tell you why he wants the cards," I said, looking at Davy.

"I want to do the cards, too," he said.

"Instead of grabbing cards from your partner, tell her that you would like to help," I suggested. "That way, she'll know. There's a way that both people can be involved." Luisa gave Davy some cards to sort.

Across the table from Davy and Luisa, Natalya was doing all of the sorting of the cards. Her partner Dean was glad to let Natalya do the work. I suspected that Natalya had tried to involve him, and I decided not to intervene.

Lea and Mitch were involved in playing the game as I came to their table. I knew that these two children knew most of the number facts and would easily know the options available for removing cards for any sum they rolled.

"Do you think there's a strategy for winning this game?" I asked them.

"Probably," Lea answered, "but I don't know yet."

"I'm trying to use one of each number and save one of each just in case," Mitch said.

"I'll be curious to see if that works," I said.

As I watched Jack and Rachel play *The 1 to 10 Game,* I noticed that they always removed cards that matched what they rolled. For example, if they rolled 4 and 2, they removed a 4 and a 2 from their hand; if they rolled 3 and 5, they removed a 3 and a 5. I wasn't sure whether they didn't fully understand the rules or they just chose to take the easy way and avoid adding. I decided to observe some more.

NOTE Whenever possible, ask children to explain what they're doing. This gives you the chance to learn what individual students understand and makes thinking and talking a natural part of students' math learning.

Soon Jack rolled 5 and 6. He had no more 5s in his hand. He looked at Rachel and said, "I can't make it."

He was about to roll the dice again when I asked, "What does 5 plus 6 equal?" Jack thought for a while and finally said 11.

"Is there another way you can make 11 besides 5 and 6?" I asked.

"You could use 10 and 1," Rachel suggested.

"Yes, and there are some other ways to make 11. Stop your game for just a minute and work together to write down other ways to make 11 with two cards. So far, you know 5 + 6 and 10 + 1," I told them. "I'll be back to check in a few minutes."

When I returned to Jack and Rachel a bit later, they had written on their paper: *5 + 6 = 11, 10 + 1 = 11, 9 + 2 = 11, 8 + 3 = 11*. "Do you think you've found all the ways of adding two numbers to make 11?" I asked. They nodded somewhat tentatively.

"I think there's one more way to make 11 with two numbers," I said.

The children studied their paper. Rachel said, "Oh, I know. It's 7 plus 4," and she wrote this on their paper.

"Remember," I said, "if you can't make the number exactly the way you rolled it, there may be other possibilities. Don't forget, you may also use three numbers."

A Class Discussion

After all of the children had played *The 1 to 10 Game* a number of times, I had a brief class discussion. "Is this a game that uses strategy, chance, or both?" I asked.

"It's kinda both," Nathan offered.

"In what way is it chance?" I asked him.

"Well," he said, "it's chance because you can't control the dice."

"Yeah, you don't know what will come up," Timothy added.

"What does it mean to have a strategy?" I asked.

"It means you think about it, like what to do," Luisa said.

"A strategy is like a plan," Mario added.

"It means you think and try to figure out what to do," Lea said.

"What are some of the strategies you've been using when you play *The 1 to 10 Game?*" I asked the class.

"I always try to save the little numbers and use the big numbers first," Mario said.

"My strategy is to use two cards every time," Luisa said.

"I try to use three cards until I run out," Yasmine said.

I concluded the discussion with a comment. "The next time you play the game, you may want to try Mario's or Luisa's or Yasmine's strategy. Or maybe you'll think of other strategies to try."

MENU ACTIVITY

Overview

Invent a Game

In this activity, students work in pairs to invent games that use dice, playing cards, or both. First, the class discusses what makes a good game, continuing the discussion that began after students played *The New Plus and Minus Game*. (See page 59.) Using the format suggested by the menu task, the class writes directions for a game the children already know. Later, the children use this format to write directions for games they invent. They spend the last two days of the unit playing games invented by their classmates.

184

Invent a Game [P]

You need: Dice

Playing cards

1. Think of a new game you could play using dice or playing cards or both.

2. The game should include adding or subtracting or both.

3. Write the directions so someone else can follow them. Tell:

    Number of players
    What you need
    How to set up
    How to play
    How to win

4. Give your game a name.

5. Have a pair of students test your directions.

From *Math By All Means: Probability, Grades 1–2*   ©1996 Math Solutions Publications

---

Before the lesson

Gather these materials:
■ Dice
■ Playing cards
■ Blackline master of menu activity, page 184

Getting started

■ Talk to the class about what makes a game enjoyable. List students' ideas on the board.

■ Together read the directions for *Invent a Game.*

■ List on the board the five categories that students should include in their games: number of players, what you need, how to set up, how to play, and how to win. To model how to use the format, have the class help you rewrite the directions for *The New Plus and Minus Game.*

■ Have children work in pairs to invent games and write the directions. Tell them to be sure to ask other students to test their directions for clarity.

■ At the end of the unit, have one or two game days so the children can play games invented by their classmates.

FROM THE CLASSROOM

"When you played *The Plus and Minus Game,* you had strong opinions about it," I began. "You knew it wasn't a game children would want to play. Today I want you to think about what makes a *good* game—one children would enjoy playing."

"It's got to be fun," Davy said emphatically. I wrote on the board:

Fun.

Then I asked, "What makes a game fun?" The students looked a little perplexed, so I tried again, "Why was *The Plus and Minus Game* not fun?"

"Because one player always won," Chris offered.

"Then what makes a good game?" I asked.

"When both players have a chance to win," Kirk said

"Yeah," several others agreed. I wrote on the board:

All players have a chance to win.

"What else?" I asked.

"I know," Mario said. "It's a game that's not boring." I wrote:

Not boring.

"Some games are too easy," Lea said.

"And some are too hard," Jack quickly added. I wrote:

Not too hard, not too easy.

I turned the children's attention to the enlarged directions for *Invent a Game.* We read them together, and I could feel the excitement. When the topic is games, all of the children become more animated. Now the thought of making up their own games had them on the edges of their seats.

To model for the students how to write directions for their games, I asked how many remembered how to play *The New Plus or Minus Game.* Almost every hand went up.

"Let's write the directions for that game so that someone who didn't know how to play it could learn," I said. "Let's follow the categories on the menu activity. I think doing this will help make the directions complete and clear and help you learn how to write directions for your own game." I wrote the following categories on the board:

Number of players
What you need
How to set up
How to play
How to win

Working together, we quickly wrote the directions. This is what we wrote:

The New Plus and Minus Game

Number of players: 2

What you need: 2 dice, paper, and pencil

How to set up: Put your names on the top of the paper. Put the title. Talk to your partner about who is Player 1 and who is Player 2. Write:

Player 1   Player 2

How to play:
1. Each player rolls one die.
2. If Player 1 gets the higher number, they get to add the two numbers and take that score. If Player 2 gets the higher number, they get to subtract. If both players roll the same number, Player 2 adds that total to their score.
3. Roll 10 times.

How to win: Add the score. Whoever gets the highest wins. Luck will help you win.

Lea raised her hand. "You need to write what age the game is for," she said.

"Hmmm, I didn't think about that," I responded.

The class became very interested in this issue. They all started shouting out ages. I told them that they could include a recommended age on their own games if they wanted to.

I gave a few additional directions. I told the students to be sure to include information for all of the categories and to be very specific when they wrote their directions. And I pointed out that the directions called for having other students test their directions before they finalized their games.

Observing the Children

Some of the children's games were complicated, and the process of writing them down became tedious. For some children, I suggested ways to simplify their games. For a few others, I wrote down their directions as they described them to me.

I watched Cindy and Yasmine play the card game they had invented. They had taken out the face cards and dealt the remaining cards so that each had 20. They both had difficulty holding the 20 cards in their hands.

Their game also involved one die. Each girl took turns rolling the die and removing a card equal to the number rolled. I was curious what they would do when they had used up all of their ace through 6 cards. I made a note to come back in a few minutes.

When I returned to Cindy and Yasmine a while later, they were still happily taking turns rolling the die and not removing any cards. I noticed that both of them had used up their ace through 6 cards. I wondered how long they would continue to roll before they noticed this fact. After each had taken two more turns, I couldn't control myself.

"What numbers are on the die that you're rolling?" I asked.

They stopped to think. Then, while moving the die around, they said, "1, 2, 3, 4, 5, and 6."

"Do you have any 1s, 2s, 3s, 4s, 5s, or 6s in your hand?" I asked.

They both looked at their cards and said no.

"This could be a problem," I said. "Think about what you could do differently." I left them to solve the problem.

I noticed that Nathan and Timothy were partners, but each was working on a different game. After I thought about this for a minute, I decided it was okay. They both seemed fully involved.

Nathan's game was quite complicated and actually involved testing psychic abilities. He put seven cards face up in a line on the table and invited me to choose a card secretly and write it down, without letting him see the number. He rolled one die and got a 3. He said, "I can take one, two, or three cards away, but I don't want to take away the card you wrote down." He removed two of the seven cards and asked, "Is your card still in the line?"

"Yes," I told him.

He rolled the die again and a 5 came up. "You can take away that amount or less," he reminded me. He cautiously removed two more cards and asked, "Is your card still there?"

"Still there," I said.

He rolled the die and got a 2. He cautiously removed one more card and asked, "Is your card still there?"

"Yes," I told him, amazed that he hadn't removed my card yet.

"Now, I can try to guess which card you wrote down," he told me. There were an 8 and a 3 left face up. Nathan looked me in the eye and guessed 3. I had picked the 8.

"That was close," I said. "Does that mean I win?"

"Yes," he said.

"I notice that your game does not include adding or subtracting," I said. "Is there a way you can put addition or subtraction into your game?"

Nathan thought for a moment and said, "You could add up the cards." He shuffled and put seven new cards face up in a line. "You add up the seven cards and whoever wins gets the points."

Nathan's game, Guess My Card, had a psychic element to it.

> Invent a game
>
> Guess My Card
>
> ① Use 1 deck of cards Ace through 10 only. Take out face cards. Shuffle ② Set 7 cards up in one line face up. Together add cards ③ Your partner picks a card and secretly writes it down.
> ④ Roll 1 die and take away that amount or less of the 7 cards but do not take away the card you think the other person wrote down.* ⑤ Do this until 1 or 2 cards are left then guess the secret card.
> ⑥ If you guess the secret card you get the points if not the score is zero.
> ⑦* If you take away the other players card he gets the points.

"That sounds good," I said.

As I walked around the room, several children were happily playing their own games. I noticed that none of them had started writing the directions. Since they were inventing as they played, they needed time to settle on one version of their game and become more familiar with the procedures.

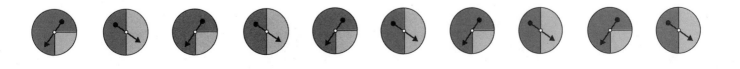

If they had a firm grasp of how to play their game, then writing the directions should be easier.

For good final directions, I had to sit with most pairs of students and edit their drafts with them. This was time-consuming but valuable. Also, even though the children had a format, not all stuck to it, and I didn't always insist. The important thing was for them to communicate their directions so I could understand them.

Matt managed to weave his interest in the solar system into the rules for his game, which was a variation on the popular children's card game Go Fish. He wrote: *When you get some cards, the first player has to start. He has to say solar system, then a number. If Player 2 has that number Player 1 gets to take that card. If Player 2 doesn't have that number Player 2 gets to say a planet.* Matt included math in his directions by having players add their cards at the end of the game.

Matt's Solar System was similar to Go Fish.

> Solar System
>
> The list of planet
> Mercury Venus, Earth
> Mars Jupiter Saturn
> Uranus Neptune Pluto.
>
> You need a deck of cards. Take out the Jacks, Queens and Kings. You have to pass out the cards. When the person has 7 cards then you can play. Each person has to take out all the matches. This is how to play. When you get some cards, the first player has to start. He has to say solar system, then a number.

> If Player 2 has that number Player 1 gets to take that card. If Player 2 doesn't have that number Player 2 gets to say a planet. This is how to win. If you have the mostes card they will win but we are still not finsh. First when your doen you could add them up. The highest number wins

Carla's game borrowed from the classic game Concentration. After laying out cards in a 3-by-3 grid, players were to follow these directions: *when one person gets a higher number, that person gets to turn over any two cards on the sides. When someone gets a pair, take two cards from the middle and replace the two cards that made the pair. When there are no more pairs, it is the end of the game.* Players added up their cards to find the winner.

Carla's game, Around the Pile, involved dice, matching cards, and addition.

> ## Around the Pile
>
> First you get two dice and a deck of cards. Then you put the cards like this ▦ and put the rest of the cards like this ▦. Then both people roll one die. When both people roll the same number, you roll again and when one person gets a higher number, that person gets to turn over any two cards on the sides. When someone gets a pair, take two cards from the middle and replace the two cards that made the pair. When there are no more pairs, it is the end of the game. When it is the end of the game, both players add up their cards. The one with the highest number wins.
>
> All the numbers are that amount of points. Aces are 1, Jacks are 11, Queens are 12 and Kings are 13

Cindy carefully followed the format for describing her game. Hers was one of the few that didn't involve playing cards. She wrote: *You have to roll the four die and put the numbers on your piece of paper. Play it about 5 time. When your don add up your score. Who every has the highest score wins.*

Unlike most students, Cindy didn't use playing cards in her game.

> ## The Die Game
> Ages 5 and up
>
> you need 4 dies and paper, pencil
>
> How many players 2
>
> How to play
> You have to roll the four die and put the numbers on your piece of paper. Play it about 5 time. When your don add up your score. Who every has the highest score wins.
>
> How to win
> Try to get all 6.

Game Event

Instead of having a class discussion about their games, I decided to have a game day as a culminating event for the unit. Actually, it turned out to be two days.

The children had worked hard on their games and were eager to share them. Since they couldn't play all the games at once, I had the children on one side of the classroom host the children on the other side. Most had developed their games with partners, so six games were offered the first day and seven games the next.

I had each pair of children tell the name of the game and give a brief description. Then the class spread out around the room, some sitting on the rug and others at the back table. The children were able to play two or three different games that day. We did the same the following day, giving the other half of the children a chance to share their games.

In many cases, the children did not bother reading the directions. The inventors taught the game and told the rules as they were needed. I had the feeling that many students changed rules or invented new ones as they went along, but I didn't intervene except when students needed help.

Lea and Fredric's game, which required mental arithmetic, was a class favorite.

> 5   10   15   20
> yellow green red blue
>
> The Tile Game
>
> You should tack it like this.
>
> blue
> red
> green
> yellow
>
> The yellow worth 5 points the greens worth 10 points the reds worth 15 points and the blue worth 20 points. Each person rolls a dice and who ever has the highest number gets the tile on the bottom. You need six tile of each color and two dice. When all the yellows are gone then you take a green when all the greens are gone then you take a red when all the reds are gone then you take a blue when all the blues are gone then you add your score. If you get a double you both get one. If there is 1 more red and you get a double you roll agian.

Lea and Fredric's game was for two players and used dice and six stacks of four different colored Color Tiles. Yellow tiles were worth 5 points, green were worth 10, red 15, and blue 20. Their directions illustrated how to stack the tiles into six piles with yellows on the bottom, then green, red, and blues on the top.

Their directions for "How to play": *Each person rolls a dice, and who ever has the highest number gets the tile on the bottom. You need six tile of each color and two dice. When all the yellows are gone then you take a green when all the greens are gone then you take a red when all the reds are gone then you take a blue when all the blues are gone then you add your score. If you get a double you both get one. If there is 1 more red and you get a double you roll agian.*

Lea and Fredric's game was a popular one and, since it involved mental arithmetic, I was interested in having others play it often. Lea felt so good about her success that she invented two more games.

The excitement in the room during the game days was obvious. Children love playing games, especially when the games are their own inventions. Even though some of the games were more interesting than others, everyone's game was played, and the children were respectful. The children had worked hard over the course of the unit, and they had worked hard to complete their games in time for the game day. They were pleased with themselves and pleased with their accomplishments.

CONTENTS

HOMEWORK

Homework assignments help children continue their exploration of probability and help teachers communicate with parents about the mathematics their children are learning in school.

Since the study of probability has only recently become a part of the elementary school curriculum, most parents did not experience it as part of their elementary education. For this reason, it's vital that parents be informed about and included in what their children are doing. Through their experience with their children in school, they can learn about probability and how their children are learning about it.

Five homework suggestions are suggested. These activities are natural continuations of activities done in class. Your students may also be interested in doing other activities for homework; the best explorations come from ideas and questions posed by the children.

Each homework assignment is presented in three parts:

Homework directions

The directions explain the assignment and include organizational suggestions when needed.

The next day

This section gives suggestions for using the assignment in the classroom. It's important that children know that work done at home contributes to their classroom learning.

To parents

A letter to parents explains the purpose of the homework and the ways they can participate in their child's learning. These communications give parents information about their child's mathematics instruction.

HOMEWORK   Empty the Bowl

This homework should be assigned after the whole class lesson *Empty the Bowl.* (See page 22.)

Homework directions

Ask the children to teach someone at home how to play *Empty the Bowl.* They should use 12 tiles or other objects and one die. Lend a die to each child who does not have one at home. Tell the children that each time they play the game, they should keep track of the numbers and record how many rolls it takes to empty the bowl. Ask the children to bring their results (and the die, if they borrowed one) to school the next day.

The next day

Post the class chart for *Empty the Bowl.* Have the children record how many rolls it took for each game by placing a tally mark next to the number on the class chart. Discuss how many rolls it typically took to empty the bowl with 12 tiles and how the data changed when additional information was added.

To parents

> Dear Parents,
> The game *Empty the Bowl* gives children opportunities to add, predict results, and interpret statistics. Your child's homework assignment is to teach the game to someone at home. To play, put 12 Color Tiles or other objects in a bowl, roll one die, and take out that many objects, continuing until the bowl is empty. Your child should keep track of each number rolled. When the bowl is empty, your child will add the numbers that came up and count the number of rolls it took to empty the bowl.
> Please play at least one game of *Empty the Bowl* with your child. In class tomorrow we will collect the results and discuss them. By examining the results from many games, the children will try to determine how many rolls it typically takes to empty the bowl.

HOMEWORK   Is It 12?

This homework should be assigned after students have completed and discussed the whole class lesson *Is It 10?* (see page 32) and collected data for the menu activity *Is It 12?* (see page 83).

Homework directions

For this assignment, if children don't have playing cards at home, have them each make four sets of 1–10 cards. Ask all of the children to teach someone at home to play *Is It 12?* and to play it at least once with that person. The children should keep track of their results the same way they did for the menu activity, making a chart with the headings shown below:

<u>Less than 12</u> | <u>Exactly 12</u> | <u>Greater than 12</u>

Instruct the children to bring their results to class the next day.

The next day

Post a large sheet of chart paper and have the children record how many times they turned over two cards whose sum totaled less than 12, exactly 12, and greater than 12. Discuss the results and compare these results to the original class chart for *Is It 12?*

Ask the class: Does this new data change your thinking about what is likely when you play *Is It 12?* If we put all of our data together, what would happen to our original theory that we most likely would get less than 12?

To parents

> Dear Parents,
> As part of our probability unit, our class has played two games to try to determine what sums are likely when you turn over two cards from a deck with four sets of 1–10 cards. First, we played *Is It 10?* trying to find out if the sums were likely to be less than, equal to, or greater than 10. Our data indicated that we were more likely to get a sum that was greater than 10. Now we are playing the game *Is It 12?* From our class sample so far, sums less than 12 seem more likely. We want to collect more data for our class chart so that we have a larger sample of data to analyze. Your child's homework assignment is to teach *Is It 12?* to someone at home and to play the game to collect more data.
>
> Playing this game also gives your child practice with basic addition facts. I hope that you will enjoy playing *Is It 12?*

HOMEWORK

Spinners

This homework should be assigned after the menu activity *More Spinners* (see page 117) and the assessment *100 Spins* (see page 127).

Homework directions

Have the students take home the spinner they made for *More Spinners* and ask someone at home to help them spin the spinner and record the results. The children should spin 25 times, keep track of the colors the spinner lands on, and bring in their results the next day.

The next day

Have the students gather in groups of four and combine their spinner results. Ask each group to report how many times the spinner landed on blue and how many times on red during the total 100 spins. Record this information and discuss the results.

To parents

> Dear Parents,
> As part of our probability unit, the students made spinners that they colored $\frac{3}{4}$ blue and $\frac{1}{4}$ red. They collected data about the colors the spinner landed on, and then they predicted what would happen if they spun their spinners 100 times.
>
> Please help your child collect additional data by spinning the spinner 25 times and recording the results. Tomorrow, your child will combine these results with three other children. Together they will have information for 100 spins. We can't wait to see what happens!

HOMEWORK

Roll Two Dice

This homework should be assigned after the menu activity *Roll Two Dice.* (See page 132.)

Homework directions

Give each child a recording sheet to take home. Lend each child who does not have dice at home a pair to use. Review the directions for *Roll Two Dice,* and tell the children to play the game with someone at home. The children should bring their results (and dice, if they borrowed them) to school the next day.

The next day

Have each child add a tally mark to the class chart next to the number that reached the Finish Line on his or her recording sheet. Ask the students to look at the class results and discuss whether they are different now that more tally marks have been added to the chart.

To parents

> Dear Parents,
> Our class is collecting data from rolling two dice to try to determine what sums are more likely to come up on the dice than others. We need to collect more data for our class chart, as larger samples give more reliable information than smaller samples.
>
> Your child's homework assignment is to teach the game to someone at home. Please play *Roll Two Dice* with your child. He or she will roll the dice and record the two numbers that occur as an addition sentence below the sum on the recording sheet. The game ends when one sum reaches the Finish Line. This activity gives children repeated practice with basic addition facts as they collect data for our probability investigation.
>
> Thank you for helping us collect more data.

HOMEWORK

The 1 to 10 Game

This homework should be assigned after the menu activity *The 1 to 10 Game.* (See page 148.)

Homework directions

Ask the students to teach someone at home how to play *The 1 to 10 Game.* They will need a deck of playing cards (or four sets of cards numbered from 1 to 10) and a pair of dice. They should play several times and try testing a strategy to see if it helps them win.

The next day

Have the children report their experiences playing the game at home, telling with whom they played and any new strategies they discovered.

To parents

Dear Parents,
The 1 to 10 Game was invented by two second grade students when they were studying probability. The game uses cards and dice and gives children the opportunity to think about different ways to add numbers to get sums. Since dice are used, this game has the element of chance. Having a strategy, however, can increase the chances of winning. By playing the game many times, children become aware that when you roll two dice, certain sums are more likely to come up than others. Being aware of this fact can affect decisions about what cards to use first and what cards to keep for later use. Our class has just begun to talk about possible strategies.

Your child's homework assignment is to teach someone at home how to play *The 1 to 10 Game.* I invite you to play a few games with your child.

BLACKLINE MASTERS

The blackline masters fall into several categories:

Probability Menu

This blackline master lists the titles of all the menu activities suggested in the unit. You may choose to enlarge and post this list as a class reference for the work to be done. Some teachers have children copy the list and make tally marks when they do tasks; other teachers duplicate the blackline masters for individual children or for pairs of children.

Menu Activities

Eight menu activities are included. (They also appear in the text following the "Overview" section of each menu activity.) You may enlarge and post the menu tasks or make copies for children to use. (Note: A set of classroom posters of the menu activities is available from Cuisenaire Company of America.)

Instruction Sheets

Two blackline masters give directions—one for making a book and one for making a spinner.

Recording Sheets

Four blackline masters provide recording sheets for activities. Duplicate an ample supply of each and make them available for children.

Probability Menu

☐ Empty the Bowl with 20

☐ Is It 12?

☐ Likely–Unlikely Book

☐ Roll One Die

☐ More Spinners

☐ Roll Two Dice

☐ The 1 to 10 Game

☐ Invent a Game

Empty the Bowl with 20

P

You need: A bowl with 20 Color Tiles

One die

1. One player rolls the die and removes the tiles. The number on the die tells how many tiles to take out. The other player records the number of tiles taken out.

2. Stop when the bowl is empty. (You don't have to go out exactly.)

3. Together, add the numbers you rolled. Write the total on your paper. Also record how many rolls it took to empty the bowl.

4. Play 5 games. Switch jobs, so each of you takes turns rolling the die and recording.

5. Record on the class chart the number of rolls it took for each game.

From *Math By All Means: Probability, Grades 1–2*   ©1996 Math Solutions Publications

Is It 12?

You need: A deck of playing cards

1. Use only the ace, 2, 3, 4, 5, 6, 7, 8, 9, and 10 cards.

2. Shuffle the deck and deal all of the cards so both partners have the same amount. Each player keeps the cards in a pile, face down.

3. Each player turns over the top card. Together, add the two numbers aloud. Remember that ace = 1. Decide if the total is less than 12, exactly 12, or greater than 12.

4. Record the results like this:

Less than 12	Exactly 12	Greater than 12
4 + 5 = 9	7 + 5 = 12	10 + 4 = 14

5. Continue for all the cards.

6. Count how many times the sums were less than 12, exactly 12, and greater than 12. Record the totals for each game on the class chart.

From *Math By All Means: Probability, Grades 1–2* ©1996 Math Solutions Publications

How to Make a Book

You need: 1 sheet of white construction paper
Scissors

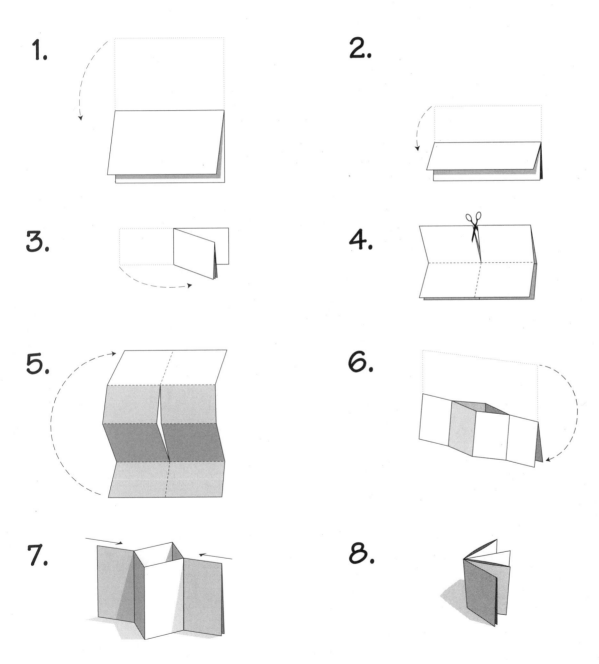

1.

2.

3.

4.

5.

6.

7.

8.

Likely-Unlikely Book

You need: 1 sheet of lined newsprint
           1 sheet of white construction paper
           Scissors

1. Use the lined paper to make a draft of your Likely–Unlikely Book. Fold the paper into 8 sections.

2. Write 4 likely statements and 4 unlikely statements, one in each box. When you finish your draft, place it in the "to be edited" box.

3. After your draft has been edited, make a book using a sheet of white construction paper. Title your book "Likely–Unlikely."

4. On each left-hand page, write one of your <u>likely</u> statements. On each right-hand page, write one of your <u>unlikely</u> statements. Draw pictures to illustrate your book.

How to Make a Spinner

You need: 1 spinner face
  1 card
  1 paper clip
  1 piece of plastic straw
  Scissors
  Tape

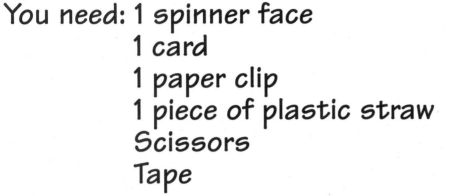

1. 2.

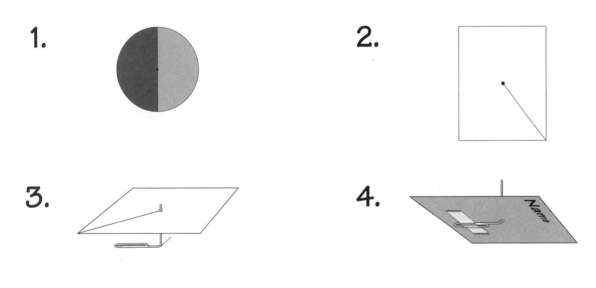

3. 4.

5. 6.

Spinner Faces #1

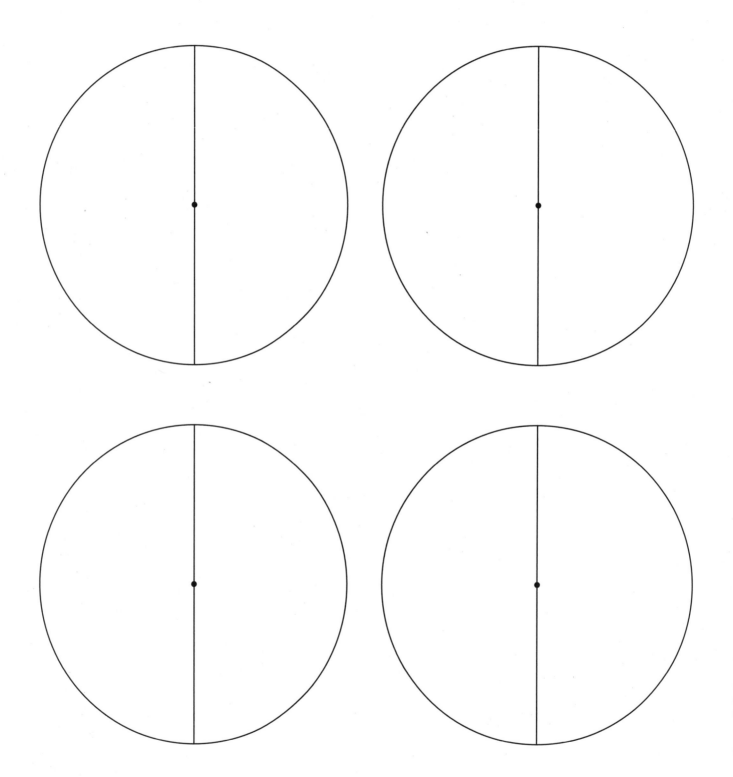

Spinner Faces #2

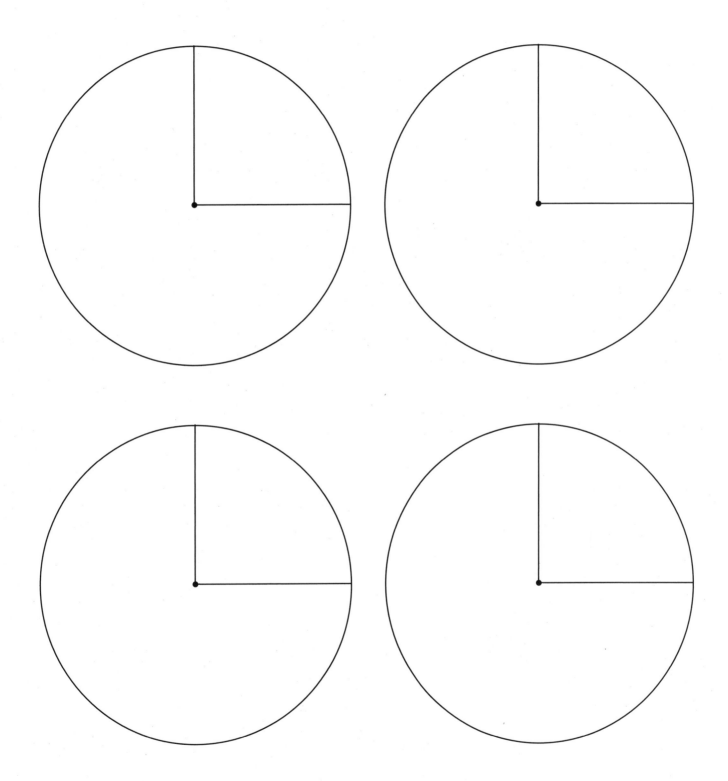

Spinner Recording Charts

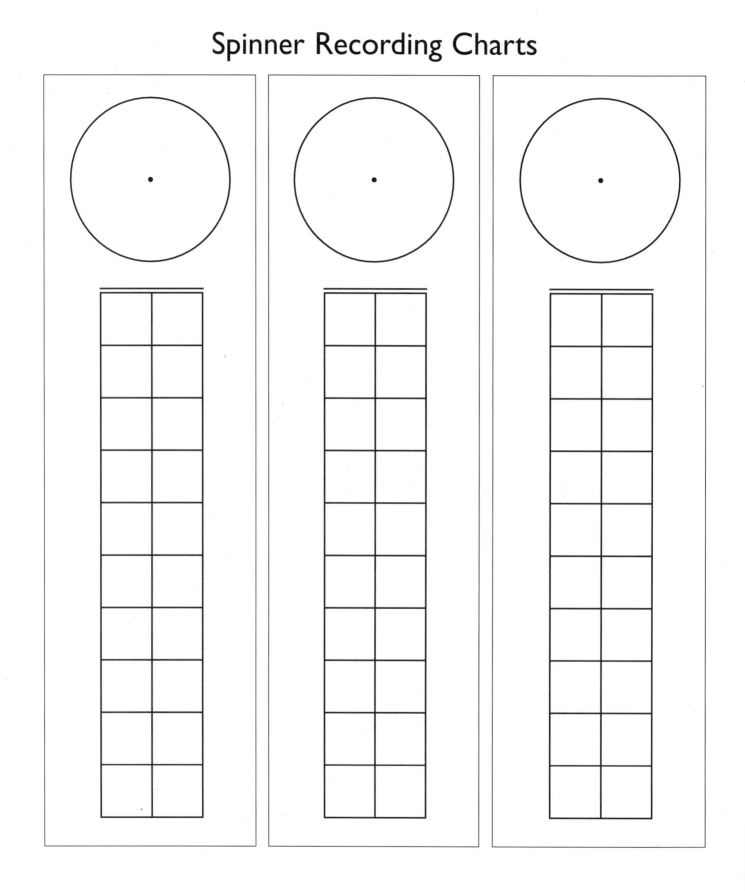

More Spinners

You need: 1 spinner with #2 spinner face
           Spinner recording chart

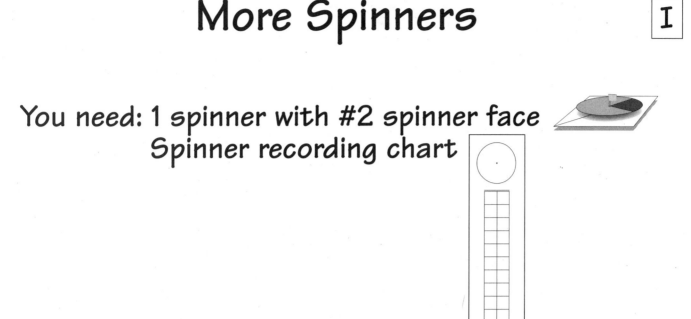

1. Make a spinner that is $\frac{1}{4}$ red and $\frac{3}{4}$ blue.

2. Tape a recording chart to a sheet of lined paper.

3. Predict: If you spin this spinner many times, what do you think will happen? Write your prediction.

4. Spin the spinner and record the color that it lands on. Spin and record until one color reaches the top of its column.

5. Write about the results.

From *Math By All Means: Probability, Grades 1–2* ©1996 Math Solutions Publications

Roll One Die

You need: One die

1. Make a chart.

Roll One Die					
1	2	3	4	5	6

2. Roll the die at least 25 times.

3. Make a tally mark to keep track of each number you roll.

4. Record the total number of rolls for each number at the bottom of each column.

From *Math By All Means: Probability, Grades 1–2* ©1996 Math Solutions Publications

Roll Two Dice

You need: 2 dice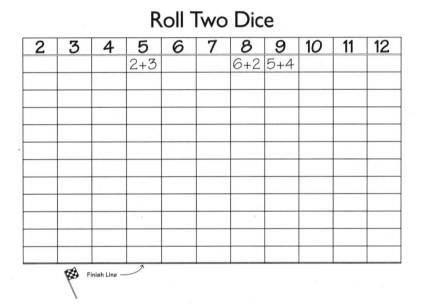
Roll Two Dice recording sheet

1. Roll two dice and record the addition sentence below the correct sum.

Roll Two Dice

2	3	4	5	6	7	8	9	10	11	12
			2+3			6+2	5+4			

Finish Line ⟶

2. Continue rolling the dice until one number reaches the Finish Line.

3. Mark a tally on the class chart to show your winning number.

From *Math By All Means: Probability, Grades 1–2* ©1996 Math Solutions Publications

Roll Two Dice

2	3	4	5	6	7	8	9	10	11	12

Finish Line

From *Math By All Means: Probability, Grades 1–2* ©1996 Math Solutions Publications

The 1 to 10 Game

P

You need: Two dice

1 deck of cards

1. Use only the ace, 2, 3, 4, 5, 6, 7, 8, 9, 10 cards.

2. One of you takes the red cards, and one of you takes the black cards.

3. Take turns. On your turn, roll the dice and figure out the sum. Remove enough cards from your hand to add up to that sum.

   For example, if you roll a 5 and a 3, you can make 8 in many ways, including:

4. If you can't make the sum with cards from your hand, roll again. If you can't make a sum after three rolls, you lose the game.

5. You win if your partner can't make a number in three rolls or if you use up all your cards.

From *Math By All Means: Probability, Grades 1–2* ©1996 Math Solutions Publications

Invent a Game

You need: Dice

Playing cards

1. Think of a new game you could play using dice or playing cards or both.

2. The game should include adding or subtracting or both.

3. Write the directions so someone else can follow them. Tell:

 Number of players
 What you need
 How to set up
 How to play
 How to win

4. Give your game a name.

5. Have a pair of students test your directions.

INDEX